PSYCLOSIS

PSYCLOSIS

THE CIRCULARITY OF EXPERIENCE

RALPH BERGER

University of California, Santa Cruz

W. H. FREEMAN AND COMPANY
San Francisco

Library of Congress Cataloging in Publication Data

Berger, Ralph.
   Psyclosis.

   Bibliography: p.
   Includes index.
    1. Experience.   2. Science—Philosophy.
3. Humanities.   4. Neurobiology.   I. Title.
BF455.B365   153'.01   77-24398
ISBN 0-7167-0018-2

Printed in the United States of America

9 8 7 6 5 4 3 2 1

Contents

Acknowledgments

I wish to acknowledge my gratitude to those many colleagues, students, and friends with whom I had lengthy discussions about the ideas in this book, and who made critical comments and constructive suggestions. Their list is too long for me to cite each individual, and I do not wish to run the risk of omitting someone whose valuable contributions I had forgotten or failed to recognize. I single out only Calvin Hall, who has also gently guided my career, and my wife, Gunnela, who patiently endured listening to my ideas on their trial runs. I dedicate this book to them both.

I am also grateful to the University of California for granting me a sabbatical leave, and the following for providing me with shelter and an environment conducive to writing: The Netherlands Central Institute of Brain Research; Michael Corner; Flory and Albert Holmgren; Lisa and Thomas Holmgren; Agnes and Robert Lyons; and the charming city of Amsterdam, where most of the book was written.

Preface

My dear friend, I send you a little work of which no one can say, without doing it an injustice, that it has neither head nor tail, since, on the contrary, everything in it is both head and tail, alternatively and reciprocally.

Baudelaire

This book is about the structure of experience (by which I mean all aspects of mental activity, including perceptions, emotions, images, ideas, thoughts, etc). Since language is a symbolic representation of experience, a written work must refer to experiences of one kind or another. It cannot transcend experience and describe an "external reality" that is independent of experience. The differences in language between intellectual disciplines reflect the different aspects of experience with which each discipline is concerned. Moreover, each discipline uses different criteria in establishing relations between experiences.

Scientific theories and literary works both deal with experience. The scientist's experiences are obtained predominately by the construction, manipulation, and observation of measuring instruments, whereas those of the novelist are obtained by the observation of people and *milieu*. Much is made of the objective nature of science and the subjective nature of the novel. But the distinction between "subjective" and "objective" lies in the degree of correspondence that exists between the experiences of individuals—the higher the degree of correspondence the greater the objectivity. Through the experimental isolation of certain events from uncontrolled influences and the observation of precise and reliable technical instruments, scientific experiences become universal.

Prior observations can be recalled through memory. The process of memory allows us to associate one memory image with another and from two memory images we can draw an infinity of relations. Since analysis constitutes an examination of relations, it follows that an analysis of experience must be either inconclusive or circular. If the analysis progressively draws new relations from an initial body of experience but does not relate all the newly established relations back to their source in the initial body of experience, it is open-ended and inconclusive. If it limits itself to the internal organization of a limited body of experience, it must necessarily be circular.

Circularity applies to most philosophical analyses, including the one I am about to present in this book. If one attempts to apply the conclusions of a particular philosophical analysis to the analysis itself, one must eventually face the fact that the system does not have any application beyond itself. One finds oneself trapped within circles of thought. To illustrate, let us take the analysis in this book. I shall examine the structure of experience in terms of certain brain processes that form the necessary conditions for experience. But "brain processes" are themselves concepts derived from experiences of scientists—obtained by observing various mechanical, electronic, optical, or chemical measuring instruments. The conclusion that brain processes are necessary conditions for experience in general is therefore circular from the standpoint of experience itself. The only alternative to this circularity is the inconclusive strategy of an endless reduction of one set of brain processes to another, more "fundamental" set.

It is sometimes argued that *sound* scientific theories are not circular because new evidence is subsequently found that is consistent with those theories. But it should be recognized that such "new" evidence is uncovered in experiments designed to test a particular scientific theory. The theory dictates the method of investigation, and the methodology in turn dictates the kinds of evidence that will be "discovered." Consequently, the evidence cannot fail to be consistent with the theory.*

Scientific theories are thought forms that relate a collection of past experiences. They act as shorthand expressions, saving memory capacity that would otherwise have to be devoted to remembering countless isolated experiences. Science relies on the development of theories, since predictions about particular future experiences are drawn from them. When the predictions are not confirmed, theories are disproved and new and more productive ones are sought.

But science is simply one example of a more general process of memory and expectation. Memory reflects the past in images, and the future is anticipated by new

---

*Theories that are falsified by empirical evidence are, by definition, unsound.

constructions derived from memory images. This *imagined* future is subsequently compared with unfolding
present perceptions and either confirmed or disconfirmed. When confirmed, these constructions known as
the future are considered to be actual and true; when
disconfirmed, they are considered to be subjective and
false. Thus the future as well as the past involves
memory—without memory neither a past or future, or
time itself, could be conceived.

Science, the humanities, and the arts are all modes of
apprehending the world; in each, past experiences are
structured in particular ways. Whereas science attempts
to understand nature by acting upon it, the humanities
and arts are satisfied to merely contemplate it. Such
contemplation may lead to works of art, but these are
made not to confirm or disconfirm any specific prediction resulting from reflection on experience, as in science. Instead, works of art are intended to act directly
on those who view them by restructuring their experiences along lines similar to those that originally occurred in the artist. This difference in intention is one of
the principal distinctions between science and other
creative enterprises.

The sciences and the humanities also differ in their
subject matter. The sciences analyze physical
phenomena, whereas the humanities analyze mental
experience. The social sciences have attempted to
bridge the two disciplines, but so far unsatisfactorily.
Clear relationships have not been established between
the two kinds of experience and we continue to be confronted with the seemingly insoluble dualism of mind
and body, and free will versus determinism.

My aim in writing this book was to analyze the scientific and humanistic modes of experience in such a way

as to integrate them. The key to achieving that aim appeared to me to lie in a consideration of the evolutionary functions of the brain, which form the necessary conditions for all experiences. The physical phenomena "described" by science are the result of particular experimental operations in which the human body and brain interact with the external world either directly or by intermediary technical instruments. Experiences of physical phenomena do not entail the existence of the physical phenomena independent of the experiences themselves. Instead, they reflect the physiological and cultural dispositions of the human brain to interact with the environment in certain ways.

By examining the nature of memory and time from a neurobiological standpoint, I found that the traditional problems of mind and body and of free will and determinism no longer presented themselves as meaningful questions. Rather than representing different aspects of an "external reality," the mental and the physical could be regarded as different *categories of experience*, which can be related to each other in terms of certain neurobiological functions of the brain. Of course the "neurobiological functions of the brain" are themselves phenomena, so that it should be clear that the philosophical approach I shall take is phenomenological.

In concerning myself with memory and time, my intention is not to offer an explanation of these concepts, but instead to analyze them in such a way that we are led to the realization of the biological relativity and essential circularity of all experience and knowledge, including that of memory and time themselves. To do so I shall consider a variety of closely related concepts, including the Second Law of Thermodynamics, organic evolution, ontogenesis, learning, reinforcement, homeostasis, perception, consciousness, dreaming, the Collective Unconscious, and the will. In relating these concepts to one another I shall take up the evolutionary approach to neural, behavioral, and experiential data begun by Mach (1943), Pearson (1951), von Bertalanffy (1969), Munéver (1975), and Stent (1975), and shall rely heavily on neo-Darwinian theory for their interpretation. This approach can be called *biological relativism*. I shall argue that a necessary condition of experience is *interaction* between the organism and the environment, so that the structure of experience reflects the structure of both the organism and the environment with which it interacts. It follows that an organism cannot experience its own structure or that of the environment independently of the other.

Since I am about to engage in a circle of thought, wherever I choose to enter the circle is arbitrary. I have chosen time and motion as my starting point. As far as possible, I have tried to avoid the use of dualistic language in reaching towards a monistic philosophical endpoint. Wherever I have failed to do so I beg the reader's indulgence.

Santa Cruz   *Ralph Berger*
June 1977

PSYCLOSIS

Time and Motion 1

Movement is a principal characteristic of life, being most pronounced in animals but also exhibited by plants as they raise and lower their leaves, open and close their petals, or turn toward the sun. Even such seemingly sedentary animals as corals are not static, since the polyps move in and out of the protective limestone skeleton that they communally secrete. Movement also exists *within* the bodies of living things, ranging from the macroscopic level, such as heartbeat and blood flow, to microscopic levels, such as the descent of auxins from the shoots toward the bases of plants.

But is movement an *essential* characteristic of life? What if we could freeze an animal and thaw it out later so that it behaved the same way as it did prior to freezing? Would we consider the animal "alive" while frozen, even when all physiological variables proved to be

absent? We might try to escape this dilemma by using
the phrase "suspended animation." Suspension of overt
movement (but not internal physiological changes) occurs naturally in such states as sleep, torpor, and hibernation. But these differ from the above hypothetical
example in exhibiting endogenous reversal to the waking state, without requiring an external change in such
variables as temperature or illumination to provoke the
reversal. In the hypothetical state of "suspended animation" the return of life would depend upon the Faustian
intervention of the experimenter.

An implicit assumption underlying the life sciences is
that the evolution, growth, and behavior of organisms
should ultimately be explainable exclusively in terms of
energy fluxes originating outside the body of the organism. But the attainment of such an explanation
would mean, paradoxically, that an organism could not
be considered any more alive than a marionette, since
both could be unequivocally shown to be driven by
specific identifiable external forces. In other words,
were we able to predict to the finest detail the motions
of certain organisms we would most certainly regard
them as automata, and our notion of "life" would simply
mean "organisms whose motions remained to be explained." Such a change in view has recently occurred
with regard to viruses, as a result of the success of
molecular biology in explaining their structure and processes of self-replication. At present, viruses represent
to us a borderland between "living" and "non-living"
matter. Clearly, our definition of life changes with the
current state of biological knowledge and level of technological development. But it should be emphasized
that the technical instruments used in scientific experiments to develop physical explanations of organismic

behavior are artificial products of human actions that themselves require physical explanations. Thus we find ourselves caught within the circle of our investigations—a situation we shall repeatedly encounter throughout this analysis.

Of course, the question "What is life?" cannot be answered by pointing to a single attribute such as motion. The phenomenon of life involves many attributes acting in concert. At this point I merely wish to call attention to the intimate association of life with motion, without trying to draw a distinction between living and nonliving matter solely on the basis of this association.

The concept of motion is inextricably linked not only with that of life, but with that of time as well. In fact, it is impossible to think of time without motion or of motion without time. One concept is always defined in terms of the other, so that they are inseparable. An analysis of the nature of time has raised inexorable difficulties for those philosophers and scientists courageous enough to attempt it. Saint Augustine expressed the problem in the well-known epigram taken from his *Confessions:* "What is time? If no one asks me, I know; if I want to explain it to someone who does ask me, I do not know." Contemporary treatises on time continue to express the same perplexities. For instance, in a review of P.C.W. Davies' book *The Physics of Time Asymmetry* John Wheeler writes (1975):

> Never has a saner book been written on a more insane subject. In every other part of physics there is reasonable consensus as to the lay of the land; but this is not so when it comes to the "arrow of time." One has only to question a dozen responsible and thoughtful physicists to find that there are two camps on the matter. No one doubts that entropy increases, stars pour out energy, evolution moves

forward in time and memory contains only the past—and that all this development goes on while the universe is expanding. But the evidence is powerful that the expansion of the universe is slowing down and that there is truth in Einstein's views that this expansion will come to a halt and be followed by a phase of contraction.

As dynamic time marches forward, what will happen then to statistical and biological time? Will they continue to point in the same direction or will they point in opposite directions? In the one case, to a person alive in the second phase of the universe, the universe will appear to be contracting. In the other case, it will appear to be expanding, simply because a moving picture of contraction run backwards looks like expansion. Many colleagues agree that the question is open and that the answer is one of the great puzzles of our day; but others are strongly convinced that the one answer or the other is the only right answer and that the answer is perfectly obvious and should be accepted without question. This is the insanity of the subject. [p. 49]

My aim here is not to engage in an exhaustive discussion of the complexities involved in any satisfactory explanation of time, but instead to focus on those aspects of time that indicate that a complete explanation of time cannot be rendered by invoking only concepts referring exclusively to physical events, but must also include certain biological and psychological concepts. Bergson (1910) showed how meaningful descriptions of nature implicitly include the connotation of time as *duration* within them. Although we can abstract the idea of an instant of time from our perceptions of nature in terms of coincidences between certain events, if we then try to describe nature as a *series* of instantaneous events we effectively introduce duration into the description. Time itself connotes the idea of the instant in conjunction with that of duration. Georgescu-Roegen (1971) elaborates this point in the following manner:

In a nutshell, the position of Whitehead and Bergson is that Time is filled with events that endure and overlap in a dialectical succession. Above all, Time is not a sequence, however dense, of durationless instants representable by numbers. The reason why this simplistic scheme exercises nevertheless such a great fascination even on some professional philosophers is that we all have the tendency to think of instants rather than duration in relation to Time. Whether as physicists in a laboratory or as ordinary people going about our business, we are preoccupied primarily with coincidences—the coincidences of a clock's hand with one of the points on the dial. "It is half past three and he has not shown up yet," or "I was just leaving when the telephone rang," are typical of our way to notice Time. We rarely pay conscious attention to the flux of Time, and even when we do, more often than not we again refer to coincidences.

When we observe motion we also focus our attention on coincidences, the passage of the moving body through some place or other. And as Bergson observes, we thus imagine that the moving body *"might* stop there; and even when it does stop there, [we] incline to consider its passage as an arrest, though infinitely short, because [we] must have at least the time to think of it." This is how we get the illusion—against which Zeno aimed his paradoxes—that motion consists of a sequence (dense, to be sure) of rests. Nothing need be added to bring to the surface the full incongruity of the entirely equivalent position that Time is nothing but a dense sequence of durationless instants. [pp. 70–71]

This is the conception of time I shall adopt here. It is also the one adopted in physics, where operational procedures for its measurement are specified. Any such specified procedure for measuring time constitutes the definition of a "clock" and its corresponding "time scale."

The concept of the clock in turn rests on the rationale that one interval of time as measured by a relation between two events, such as two different positions of a clock's hands, is the same as another subsequent interval as measured by the same relation between two similar events. This rationale constitutes a basic philosophical principle of physics, as expressed by James Maxwell (1952): "The difference between one event and another does not depend on the mere differences of the times or the places at which they occur, but only on the differences in the nature, configuration, or motion of the bodies concerned."

In other words, the behavior of matter is considered constant over time, so that the events that recur in scientific experiments in which all conditions are held constant except for displacements in time or space are regarded as the same. Physics involves the study of those properties of matter that are *uniform*, without relation to history. The behavior of matter is described by a system of differential equations in which time does not enter explicitly, so that the laws of dynamics are symmetrical with respect to time reversal. The major exceptions to this general principle are the physical phenomena of hysteresis and thermodynamics. I shall discuss the question of time and the irreversibility of thermodynamic events shortly. In the case of hysteresis, although a historical factor is involved, it differs from that involved in biology and the social sciences. The history of a magnet can be effectively eliminated by demagnetizing it (and does not functionally exist for a piece of nonmagnetized iron), whereas initial zero conditions of history cannot be reestablished in the biological sciences, which rest on the theory of evolution (Georgescu-Roegen, 1971). In physics the initial conditions necessary for the subsequent appearance of certain phenomena in accordance with basic laws can be repeated at will. Thus, magnets with the same history behave in the same way. In the biological and social sciences we do not have the ability to experimentally repeat initial conditions in the same way, especially in light of the fact that we ourselves represent part of the total system we are trying to understand.

Since, with the exceptions of the phenomena just noted, physics is concerned with those properties of matter that do not change with time, it was possible for Einstein to conceive of time in the same way as space such that events could be set in a four-dimensional space–time manifold. By means of the Lorentz transformations, events perceived by one observer in an inertial system can be related to those perceived by another observer in an inertial system moving relative to the first system, so that the same dynamic laws apply to events as witnessed from within either inertial system. In this way relativity theory led to a conception of a universe of physical events that could be represented by a system of equations whose spatial and temporal coordinates could be transformed from one observer to another observer moving relative to the first. In effect the Lorentz transformations constitute a kind of communication system between observers so that their individual measurements of physical events are in agreement even though each observer is located at a different temporal and spatial point within the universe.

But although the spatial vector representation of time in relativity physics constituted a radical change in the description of universal events, it did not lead to a different conception of time itself. The spatial vector of time is represented by the distance a ray of light travels *in a given time*. Since light is assumed to travel at constant velocity in empty space independent of the motion of its source, time could thereby be represented as a geometric distance measured in light meters, i.e., one second would be represented by the distance traveled by light in one second (3×10^8 meters). Nevertheless, although time can be represented as a distance in this way, the actual measurement of that distance must at some point involve the use of a clock. Thus the space–time of relativity physics represents a formal mathematical operation and does not eliminate the fundamental differences in the practical operations involved in the measurement of distance and time.

The ability to transform a temporal measurement into a distance rests on the assumption that the velocity of light is constant. But, as anticipated by Poincaré, relativity theory has demonstrated the impossibility of determing an absolute velocity. It follows that the absolute rate at which changes occur (assumed to apply uniformly to all events, including our own bodily processes) cannot be determined since all mechanical phenomena are parallel in their ensemble. As Georgescu-Roegen (1971) puts it:

> . . . any temporal law of pure physics is nothing but the enunciation of a temporal parallelism between two mechanical phenomena, one of which is a mechanical clock. From this it follows that all mechanical phenomena, including that of a clock, are parallel in their ensemble. In principle, therefore, we could choose any such phenomena to serve as the common basis for the enunciation of parallelism.
>
> . . . physics offers no proof that the clock hour just elapsed is equal to the one just beginning (Pearson, 1937). Time intervals cannot be superimposed so as to find out *directly* whether they are equal. Nevertheless, we have a

strong feeling that they are, that Time flows at a constant rate hour by hour—as Newton taught. [p. 137]

But relativity theory argues that this feeling of uniformity in the passage of time is an illusion and that in different inertial systems in relative motion clocks run at different speeds. However, they would not be *perceived* as running differently by an observer moving from one system to another, since all mechanical phenomena (including the observer's brain processes) would undergo the same transformation in their speed as do the clocks. Only if consciousness were independent of physical events occurring in both the brain and the environment would there be any difference in the perception of the rate of passage of time. But there is some evidence that the conscious perception of duration is inversely correlated with the rate of metabolism (Hoagland, 1933) so it is unlikely that we could ever obtain any experiences that would allow us to determine an absolute rate at which mechanical changes occur, or even whether that rate itself is uniform. The possibility can be conceived that, relative to a hypothetical observer in another universe, everything in our universe is running at a progressively faster rate. But as long as any such progressive increase in rate were uniform for all mechanical phenomena we would have no way of knowing it.

The measurement of time by means of an ideal clock, therefore, rests on the assumption that the behavior of the clock is uniform. This ideal is more fully realized by periodic clocks involving cyclic variations, such as the oscillations of a pendulum, balance wheel, quartz crystal, or of atoms, than it is by clocks involving linear changes, such as water, sand, or candle clocks. Although periodic clocks do eventually wear out with time, the rate at which their cycles occur is less affected by the number of cycles that have already occurred than the rate of change of events in a linear clock is affected by such previous events as how much water or sand has already passed through it. Of course, linear clocks can be calibrated by means of periodic clocks (paradoxically yielding nonlinear measurement scales), but then the periodic clock becomes the standard measuring instrument. Thus, time is measured by counting the number of cyclic changes in the appearance of some object, such as the rising and setting of the sun, or the oscillation of an atomic clock.

Cyclic change occurs not only in the physical world, it also constitutes a cardinal characteristic of living organisms. It is present at every level in both plants and animals. One can probably safely say that there does not exist a physiological variable that does not exhibit cyclic variation. In animals we can observe cyclic changes ranging from one millisecond (in nerve action potentials) to one year (in neuroendocrine processes involved in migration, hibernation, and sexual and reproductive functions). Even the birth, life, and death of organisms constitute a cyclic process.

The topic of "biological clocks" has attracted considerable interest in recent years and is derived from observations of the persistence of remarkably stable cyclic events in animals and plants even when experimentally isolated from all known cyclic changes in their physical environment. Thus, plants continue to raise and lower their leaves and hamsters continue to sleep and run in activity wheels in constant light or darkness, but with a period of alternation that is slightly longer or shorter than 24 hours. When decoupled from the natural environment these ongoing rhythms are known as "free-running" rhythms. They are inherited, since the offspring of animals bred under uniform conditions also display them immediately after birth. When animals bred in a constant environment are exposed to a natural alternation of light and darkness, their innate activity–inactivity rhythms are entrained by the natural environmental changes so that the onset and offset of activity becomes closely linked with that of light and darkness and its period shifts to exactly 24 hours. Diurnal animals are entrained by light and darkness in such a manner that their activity periods begin shortly before the onset of light. Therefore, their activity is not directly triggered by the light. Instead, diurnal animals maintain an internal record of the time that has passed since darkness descended and they became inactive and fell asleep. In this way they anticipate the dawn by waking up and becoming active prior to the actual sunrise. The adaptiveness of this behavior is apparent for those diurnal animals that live in deep holes or burrows and are not exposed to the rays of the rising sun. Since the responsiveness of the brain to environmental influences such as light is considerably reduced during sleep, even those animals that sleep outside might miss the early morning if they had to rely on sunlight to awaken them. Physiological activity rhythms can be understood to have arisen by natural selection so as to maximize the potentiality of survival of the organism in a uniformly changing environment.

Because cyclic changes are inherent in all living organisms, time is necessarily involved in a description of their characteristics, which helps to explain why historicism (evolution) is valid in the life sciences, whereas in pure physics it is excluded. In other words,

since time is inherent within living systems, it can be
involved in the determination of an event. An example
of this would be the human behavior of arranging an
appointment some days in advance. The appointment,
if kept, is dependent upon each person's ability to maintain a continuous record of time by the construction of
chronometers. The act of meeting then occurs when the
chronometer reaches a critical value. In this way time
itself becomes a critical variable in the determination of
behavior.

In physics time is not considered a causal variable.
Causality in the physical world is set *in* time. Events are
considered to follow one another in time, but time itself
is not considered to be a cause of their happening as
they do, only a necessary condition for their happening.
In physics nothing can exist outside of time, and those
things that do exist, exist for reasons not connected with
time. As Kant realized, time is an *a priori* intuition
necessary for things to become apparent but does not
influence the form of appearances—much as the paper I
am writing on is necessary for the appearance of these
words but has nothing to do with the particular words
that appear on it. Time is also used in science as a
means of relating events that are not conjoined in space.
This is known as *correlation*.

The use of time in physical mechanics can be illustrated by the example of plotting the trajectory of a pro-
jectile (Figure 1). In this operation time (*t*) is not a

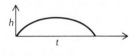

FIGURE 1

causal variable but instead is a *representational* variable in relation to height (*h*). Cause and effect constitute a sequence of events that involves a transformation of energy. Logically speaking, when we say that change (transformation of energy) *requires* time, we mean only that time is a necessary condition for change, not that it is itself a cause of change.

Time is not a quality in the physical world itself. Instead, it is *lived*. It is generated as an abstraction from successive experiences and only subsequently does it become a quality ascribed to the physical world. To put it another way, time is inherent within the living organism and its consciousness, rather than a universal aspect of the physical world. The foregoing statement is merely a reformulation in biological terms of Kant's conception of time as *a priori* intuition. Time is not experienced directly, within a momentary perception, but is abstracted from successive perceptions by comparing them through memory. The *sense* of time thus arises from within consciousness but is then projected onto the physical world, thereby undergoing the process of "objectification."*

Because of memory, experience at any moment is affected by earlier experiences. The world perceived at a given moment can also be compared with the retentional image of the world perceived a moment ago. If memory did not exist there would be only an instantaneous Now, and the experience of time itself could not arise. By way of illustration let us consider the hands of a clock. If we observe them at intervals of less than 12 hours we regard them as having moved. This

---

*For a detailed analysis of the phenomenology of internal time-consciousness and its objectification see Edmund Husserl(1964).

conclusion of course depends upon the memory that at some earlier time the hands were observed to be in a different position. However, if we observe the hands at two instants exactly 12 hours apart, the two perceptions in themselves do not yield the experience that time has passed; only the memory of intervening events yields that experience. So we can see that in the latter case time does not pertain to any physical events in the clock itself but only to those in the observer, in whom a biological clock is so to speak embedded as a matrix of innumerable physiological events. Time is derived internally and the mechanical clock and all other physical time-measuring devices are merely more accurate technological extensions of the intrinsic biological time-generator. An objection to this example might be that the clock was not in actual fact identical at the two points 12 hours apart, that parts of its cogwheels had been worn away with the passage of time. But attention is not normally directed towards these signs of wear and tear in the measurement of time, and, as was emphasized earlier, an ideal clock is one that theoretically is completely free of friction and exhibits no change in the structure of its parts with time.

The wearing-out of clocks is an example of the physical concept of entropy, which, according to the Second Law of Thermodynamics, is always increasing within the universe as a whole. The Second Law of Thermodynamics is a strictly evolutionary law that is concerned with irreversible processes with a clearly defined "arrow of time," namely, entropy. But although the Second Law ascribes directionality to the changing universe, it says nothing about the rate of change; it is not concerned with the measurement of time. If time were somehow measured by the increase in entropy, then, as Eddington (1928) pointed out, a thermometer would be a better timepiece than an atomic clock. If I were presented with a jumble of photographs of the universe taken at various moments and asked to sort them into some serial order, I could do so by arranging them in the order of increasing entropy. But the increase in entropy between any two photographs would not allow me to calculate the amount of time that intervened between them. The establishment of the direction of time by the Second Law also depends upon memory and the recognition that two different photographs represent discrete points in a continuous evolution of the universe. The "subjectivity" of both the perception of time and the concept of entropy was clearly recognized by Eddington in 1928:*

> . . . in the parallelism between entropy-gradient and "becoming" the subjective and objective seem to have got on to the wrong sides. Surely "becoming" is a reality—or the nearest we can get to a description of reality. We are convinced that a dynamic character must be attributed to the external world; making all allowance for mental imagery, I do not see how the essence of "becoming" can be much different from what it appears to us to be. On the other side we have entropy, which is frankly of a much more subjective nature than most of the ordinary physical qualities. Entropy is an appreciation of arrangement and organisation; it is subjective in the same sense that the constellation Orion is subjective. That which is arranged is objective, so too are the stars composing the constellation; but the association is the contribution of the mind which surveys. If colour is mind-spinning, so also is entropy mind-spinning—of the statistician. It has about as much objectivity as a batting average. [pp. 94-95]

---

*The term "subjective" is used by Eddington in the traditional Cartesian sense. Later in this book, when dealing with the problem of perception, I shall argue against this traditional usage.

That dynamic quality, that significance which makes a
development from past to future reasonable and a development from future to past farcical. . . , is so welded
into our consciousness that a moving on of time is a condition of consciousness. We have direct insight into "becoming" which sweeps aside all symbolic knowledge as
on an inferior plane. If I grasp the notion of existence
because I myself exist, I grasp the notion of becoming
because I myself become. It is the innermost Ego of all
which *is* and *becomes*. [p. 97]

Unlike Eddington, I do not intend to leap from the
"objectivity" of the physical world to the "subjectivity"
of the mental world when analyzing the concepts of
time and entropy. Instead, I shall try to unite the two
worlds through a consideration of brain processes.

In everyday life we tend to ascribe the passage of
time to our own consciousness rather than to the external world, as when we talk about time "passing slowly"
or "flying." The well-known phenomenon of time ap-
pearing to pass more rapidly with age also seems to give
lie to physical time. The perception of time appears to
be inversely related to the rate of bodily metabolism;
time appears to pass very slowly for children, who have
high metabolic rates, but appears to pass more rapidly
with age as bodily metabolism decreases in rate (Hoagland, 1933). If the perception of time depends upon the
existence of biological clocks within our bodies and
brains, then it is probable that it is directly linked with
metabolism.

Although time perception may be directly the result
of the evolution of biological clocks, biological clocks
themselves evolved from adaptations in response to external cyclic changes in geophysical events. The construction of mechanical clocks (including the sundial)
would be an outcome of this evolutionary organic pro-

cess, and in this way the internal sense of time becomes reified.

Prior to our knowledge of biological clocks, we anchored our experience of time onto external movements of the sun or more accurate artificial clocks that we manufactured. Having done so, we were then able to discover the physical clocks within our bodies that can now be identified as the "source" of our perception of time! From the standpoint of evolution, a similar circle is generated. Only because of the prior existence of cyclic geophysical events did internal biorhythmic cycles arise through natural selection; but only because of our biorhythms could our *knowledge* of evolution (predicated on the idea of time) have arisen. Clearly, there is no escape from these circles of thought and my purpose here is to reveal their existence, not to break them. The circle of time can be entered through the concept of time as *a priori* "intuition," or through the concept of time as a physical entity—"that which is measured by a clock." By either route, the circle discloses itself as the same.

2   Reinforcement

Let us return to the starting point of this discussion—the consideration of life and motion. An explanation is needed of how particular movements of the body (behavior) evolved so as to sustain life. Toward this end, further consideration of evolution from a thermodynamic perspective may prove useful. The neo-Darwinian theory of evolution is essentially *post hoc* in that it accounts for the present conditions of nature by historical analysis. It cannot make predictions more specific than the statement that evolutionary changes will continue to occur in the future. It does not generate any general principles according to which the course of future adaptations can be specified. When referring to natural selection and "survival of the fittest" in evolution we are talking tautologies, since we do not have any conception of what particular adaptations might be "fit" in future evolution. To say that a particular adaptation survived because it was "fit" is as empty as the statement that "nature takes its course." Not a single general principle underlying evolutionary adaptations has yet been developed. Molecular biology, despite its spectacular advances in the field of genetics, has so far only been able to demonstrate the chemical bases of the variations. Nor is it likely to do otherwise, since it is not concerned with the paths that evolution takes, but merely with the mechanics of it.

The same lack of prediction is also inherent in the Second Law of Thermodynamics, which simply states that the entropy of the universe must increase with time but without specifying the particular forms that increase will assume. An alternative form of the law is that disorder in the universe will increase—that the distribution of energy in the universe will become more uniform. But the exact pattern of change (which portions of the system will alter in which sequence) cannot be predicted.

If the motions constituting life processes were analyzed from a bioenergetic standpoint perhaps their evolutionary changes could be formulated in terms of entropy. Biological systems do not contradict the Second Law since the building up of macromolecules utilizes energy from the sun—entropy decreases in them only by virtue of the influx of solar energy. This energy is subsequently released as heat from metabolic activity during the life of the organism and from organic decomposition following death, when other organisms incorporate some of the bound energy in the form of biochemical bonds into their bodies. In viewing the entire universe we observe an inexorable increase in entropy. It is only when we focus exclusively on life on

earth that we see a backward eddy in the system of
increasing entropy in physical evolution. But why life
appears to flow against a physical current of events is
incomprehensible. Although the Second Law states that
the entropy of the universe increases with the flow of
time, it does not specify homogeneity in the rate of increase throughout the universe. It appears as though
life acts to retard the rate in the universe at large.* Lotka
(1945) formulated the principle that "evolution acts so
as to increase the total energy flux through the system."
This principle is the converse of the one just
suggested—that evolution acts so as to limit the rate of
increase in entropy. Where free energy is retarded in its
dispersal, new living forms appear.

Movements of the whole body or its internal parts (as
in blood circulation or respiration) require energy that
is obtained metabolically by breaking down biochemical bonds that constitute the body itself. The energy
expended in movement must be recouped by binding
equivalent amounts of energy available in food, if the
body is to be sustained without loss of mass. In bioenergetic terms, the existence of a bodily movement
depends upon the prior existence of an earlier movement (or movements) that yielded as much net energy
to the organism as the movement in question consumes.
From this historical perspective, the significance of any
particular behavior can only be understood in the context of a constellation of behaviors that, taken together,
constitute the life cycle of the organism. As Goldstein
(1939) argued in *The Organism*, there is a need for a

---

*The term "life" here includes human artifacts, whether they be
works of art, tools, or skyscrapers. The information stored in them is at
the expense of the energy released from fossil fuels used to power
machines or the metabolic heat released from foods by human work.

more holistic approach to behavior of this kind than that adopted by the classical school of Pavlovian reflexologists, or by latter-day behaviorists.

It follows that those behaviors that effectively increase the "dwell time" of solar energy in the body should tend to be selected and those that decrease it should tend to be eliminated. In biological terms this means that *those behaviors that act to sustain the body by maintaining homeostasis* are likely to increase the number of offspring living to reproductive maturity and therefore tend to be selected, whereas those that act in the opposite direction tend to be eliminated.*

Behavior can be of two general types: either it is directed towards the *acquisition* of energy, such as foraging or basking in the sun, or it is directed toward the *conservation* of energy already bound in the body, such as building protective shelters, parental protection, hibernation, or flight from predators. The time during which the behavior of a particular animal is capable of acquiring energy is dependent upon four factors: (a) the temporal distribution of food sources; (b) the temporal distribution of active predators; (c) the ambient temperature; and (d) the specialized physiology of the animal. Obviously these four factors act conjointly in the determination of behavior. For example, the inability of a

---

*I am using the term "homeostasis" as originally defined by Cannon (1932): "The coordinated physiological processes which maintain most of the steady states in the organism are so complex and so peculiar to living beings—involving, as they may, the brain and nerves, the heart, lungs, kidneys and spleen, all working cooperatively—that I have suggested a special designation for these states, *homeostasis*. The word does not imply something set and immobile, a stagnation. It means a condition—a condition which may vary, but which is relatively constant." Contemporary usage of the term differs from Cannon's definition when it is taken to refer to the *processes* that tend to maintain the constancy of the states, rather than to the states themselves (e.g., Thompson, 1967).

cold-blooded (poikilothermic) animal to be active at low temperatures because of the dependence of nervous processes on high temperatures links factors (c) and (d) together. By contrast, a warm-blooded (homeothermic) animal is capable of activity at any time of the 24-hour period (within limits) with regard to those same two factors by virtue of its specialized physiology.* The evolution of each species reflects different weightings of each of these four factors. Certain physiological processes whose adaptive functions appear to be concerned with the conservation of energy during periods of inactivity have evolved differently in different animals. Sleep, estivation, torpor, and hibernation are all forms of inactivity and involve conservation of energy beyond that attained by mere relaxed wakefulness (Berger, 1975).

Given that the central nervous system consumes relatively little energy compared with the rest of the body, one can understand the selective pressure in evolution for increased complexity of the nervous system. The complexity of control of behavior by the central nervous system is adaptive in acquiring or conserving more energy than would be spent by a less complex system incapable of generating equivalent behavior.

In accordance with these bioenergetic principles, simple reflexes responsive to particular stimuli, and associated with specific patterns of neural connections, evolved by the process of natural selection. These were followed by the faculty of learning, which is presumed

---

*The energetic advantages of the increased range in activity provided by homeothermy is achieved at great cost. Homeotherms utilize about three to four times more energy than poikilotherms of similar size (Bligh, 1973). Thus, the increased amounts of energy intake yielded by homeothermy simply "pay the cost" of having the homeothermic capacity.

to depend upon a certain innate plasticity of function of the neural matrix, such that novel behaviors can be emitted under constant stimulus conditions or previously learned behaviors can be emitted under novel stimulus conditions. Whether the neural plasticity associated with learning extends to the neural pathways forming the reflexes themselves, or whether it is confined to "associative" pathways whose function is to modulate or recombine neural activity in the reflex pathways, is currently unknown. Some degree of neural plasticity certainly exists in the neural pathways underlying simple reflexes, as is evident in the phenomenon of habituation, in which the vigor of a behavioral reflex progressively declines with repetition of the specific stimulus that evokes it. Regardless of the particular neural mechanisms that underlie neural plasticity, those behaviors that tend to maintain homeostasis are preserved either *phylogenetically*, by means of inherited reflexes, or *ontogenetically*, by learning, whereas those that eventuate in departure from homeostasis are eliminated either by natural selection or forgetting, respectively.

Nerve cells exist in the simplest of multicellular animals, such as coelenterates. The manner in which nerve cells first evolved can only be conjectured, since the processes by which cells in general differentiated in the evolution of multicellular organisms have yet to be delineated. According to the current status of knowledge in molecular biology, we can assume that nerve cells evolved as a result of a series of mutations involving alterations in the component groups forming the DNA molecules of some unknown organism(s) that lacked nerve cells. We may also assume that such prototypic nerve cells altered the behavior of those org-

anisms that possessed them in such a way as to en-
hance the organisms' ability to survive in comparison
with their nerveless relatives—similar organisms pos-
sessing nerve cells would thus proliferate, according to
the principles of natural selection. We can conceive of
ways in which such adaptive advantages could accrue to
those fortunate creatures that were the first to acquire
nerve cells. For example, the evolution of a chemoreceptor capable of influencing the motor activity of its
host so as to direct it towards areas containing the highest concentrations of nutrients would provide that animal with a selective advantage over relatives without
such receptors.

Parker (1917) traced out the evolutionary origins of
nerve cells into three functional types: sensory neurons,
motor neurons, and interneurons. Sensory neurons can
be subdivided into two types: exteroceptors, which are
excited by influences external to the organism, and interoceptors, which are excited by influences arising
from within the body. Sensory neurons are transducers
of the state of the environment and internal conditions
of the body; motor neurons are effectors of movement,
acting on the environment or altering internal bodily
conditions; and interneurons are coordinators of activity
in sensory and motor neurons so that the movements of
the animal are adaptive to environmental conditions.
We are also able to distinguish the three types of
neurons anatomically: a motor neuron axon terminates
in a muscle or gland; a sensory neuron terminates in a
synapse with another neuron, but is not activated by
axons of other neurons; and an interneuron is activated
by axons of other neurons while its own axon activates
other neurons.

It is unlikely that these three types of neurons
evolved independently. It is more likely that initially a

primordial sensory-motor neuron evolved, which subsequently differentiated into an exteroceptive sensory
neuron and a motor neuron (Figure 2). What adaptations

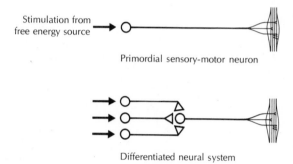

Stimulation from
free energy source ➡ Primordial sensory-motor neuron

Differentiated neural system

FIGURE 2

would accrue from such a differentiation and allow it to
be selected? One advantage is the potentiality for
amplification afforded by two types of neural elements
rather than one. Further, the convergence of several
sensory neurons upon a single motor neuron permits
increased sensitivity to sensory stimulation. It increases
the ability of an organism to detect and move towards
sources of energy. Similarly, activation of several motor
neurons by a single sensory neuron increases the vigor
of the motor response to a given level of sensory stimulation. However, sensory and motor neurons constituting such simple reflexes are unable to generate behavior characteristic of learning.

In the simple system described so far, the phenomena
of sensory adaptation and motor fatigue can occur.* But

---

*Sensory adaptation is defined as a decrease in the output of re-
ceptors in response to constant stimulation, and motor fatigue as a
decrease in muscular activity produced by constant electrical stimulation of motor neurons.

the phenomena of habituation and dishabituation depend upon the presence of the third type of neuron—
the interneuron—which current experimental evidence
indicates is located between sensory systems, as shown
in Figure 3.

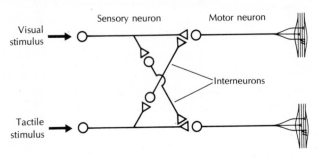

FIGURE 3

Habituation is traditionally defined by three principal criteria: (a) a progressive decrease in magnitude of
the motor response in response to repetition of the same
stimulus; (b) spontaneous recovery; and (c) dishabituation produced by presentation of a stimulus of different
intensity or of another modality. Habituation, sensory
adaptation, and motor fatigue are indistinguishable by
the first two criteria, so the third, dishabituation, is considered critical in discriminating habituation from the
other two phenomena. But dishabituation has been
shown to depend upon an underlying synaptic process of *sensitization* (Groves and Thompson, 1970;
Thompson and Spencer, 1966) so that habituation itself
is the result of some kind of synaptic adaptation. Sensitization is probably effected by interneurons forming
presynaptic facilitative connections between sensory
tracts, as shown in Figure 3 (Carew, Castellucci, and
Kandel, 1971). If a naive organism is first presented
with a visual stimulus, followed immediately by a tac-

tile stimulus, the response to the latter will be greater than if the visual stimulus had not been first presented. Accordingly, a motor response habituated by repeated presentation of a stimulus is returned to normal (i.e., dishabituated) through sensitization produced by a stimulus of another modality.

Thus sensitization is best considered as a primitive form of arousal, rather than a process exclusively involved with the *associative* properties of learning. In natural situations events are rarely restricted to one sensory modality as they are in the laboratory. Whenever a sound occurs a visual event is likely to be associated with it. Clearly, interfacilitation between sensory systems enhances the sensitivity of each and increases the ability of an animal to detect events of importance to its survival.*

Learning is commonly considered the ability of an animal to form associations between events. I propose that this ability depends on the interoceptive neuron, the second type of sensory neuron described earlier. This type of neuron could even be called the "body sensor" or "homeostasis sensor," and I intend to show how it is intimately involved in the phenomenon of reinforcement.

The concept of "reinforcement" was introduced by Skinner in connection with the concept of "operant." Both were the basis of a reconceptualization of phenomena that had been previously subsumed under the rubric "instrumental learning" and analyzed by

---

*Sokolov's (1963) studies on habituation of the orienting response and its dishabituation by the absence of one stimulus in a train of stimuli at regular intervals do not necessarily contradict the interpretation of sensitization as a form of arousal. The "absent stimulus" phenomenon has been demonstrated only in mammals and probably depends on processes of associative learning by which an animal acquires an "internal representation" of the stimulus.

Thorndike and his school according to his Law of Effect. In Skinner's system the concept of reinforcement deals more with events outside the body than with those inside, with which Thorndike was concerned (if not directly, at least indirectly). The body is not even referred to in Skinner's system, not even indirectly. The "black box" approach of behaviorism represents little more than an empirical formalization of Locke's associationism. Skinner's system attempts to relate perceptible events external to the animal through causal sequences not involving any specifications of the internal states of the organism. Skinner acknowledges this omission, but argues that although physiological events occurring within the body are necessary for learning to occur, they are not necessary for the development of scientific principles by which behavior can be predicted. Let us see to what extent this claim is justified.

A *reinforcer* is defined in Skinnerian terms as an external event that changes the probability of an operant. An *operant* is defined as a response that operates on the environment and changes it. Skinner's entire system of behavioral analysis rests on these two definitions. It should be immediately apparent that the definitions are circular, since a reinforcer is defined in terms of its effects on the probability of operants, and operants are defined in terms of their ability to affect the environment and thereby alter their own probability.* It is clear

---

*It might be argued that Skinner's two definitions are not circular because an operant could conceivably change the environment without that change having any effect on its own probability. This argument is untestable since all experiments on operant conditioning set up conditions such that the operants studied always generate external events that do in fact affect their own probability. In other words, reinforcers must always be utilized as tools in the experimental analysis since they are regarded as the only known means of controlling the behavior of an animal.

that on the basis of definitions such as these, predictions of behavior cannot possibly be made that extend to
any conditions that have not already been observed in
the past. Therefore, Skinnerian theory lacks predictive
power, as does Darwinian theory, since neither pos-
tulates any general principles according to which the
pattern of events will conform.

As I shall discuss more fully later, Skinnerian analysis
can do no more than catalog behavioral and environmental events in every conceivable combination and
thereby generate an encyclopedic index of reinforcers.
It has no application in the natural world, where evolution is occurring and the same situation never exactly
recurs. Behavioristic analysis can only make predictions
for behavior confined to the laboratory, where conditions identical to those that occurred in the past can be
artificially created. It is, therefore, entirely inductive
and is open to the same criticism as Darwinian theory,
namely, that it is in fact not a theory at all. Originally,
Skinner acknowledged this and argued against the
necessity for theories of learning, but more recently he
has openly adopted the role of a theorist (Skinner,
1969).

In contrast to the Skinnerian school of behaviorism,
many other psychologists consider the investigation of
the nervous system a necessary step in the development
of a theory of learning, since it is assumed that change
in neural efficacy must underlie learning. However,
they tend to confine their analysis of the physiology
underlying learning to the nervous system alone and
rarely consider the body as a whole. This approach
tends to disregard the potential function of learning as
producing behavior that increases the dwell-time of
solar energy in the body, as discussed earlier. For this

reason I wish to develop a model of learning that takes this function into account.

Generally speaking, learning increases the probabilities of an animal encountering situations that bring it closer to homeostasis, or of avoiding or escaping from situations that adversely affect its homeostasis. Therefore, I propose a new definition of behavioral reinforcement. *An event can be said to be reinforcing if it directly or indirectly affects bodily homeostasis.* If the change is toward homeostasis, the event is positively reinforcing; if it is away from homeostasis, the event is negatively reinforcing. What events will or will not be reinforcing are in this way defined by their effects on the entire organism rather than the brain alone.* This approach deviates from that of most contemporary neuropsychological research on reinforcement, which implicitly assumes that reinforcement resides in central processes in the brain that are primarily influenced by sensory and motor neural firing patterns. The latter approach tends to focus on the reinforcer in terms of its stimulus properties, and stems from Pavlov, who introduced the term "unconditioned stimulus" (UCS) for events that later, with the development of behaviorism, came to be thought of as "reinforcing." The reinforcer is usually considered as a stimulus in terms of its direct effects on the central nervous system rather than in terms of any general systemic effects it produces. By taking the standpoint that reinforcers help maintain the

---

*Certain learned behaviors, including curiosity, exploration, and play, do not appear to directly affect homeostasis. But, as I shall argue in due course, taken in the larger context of their effect on other behaviors that do directly affect homeostasis, this class of behaviors indirectly influences homeostasis. In the next two chapters I shall speculate that there are two types of learning: one that directly affects homeostasis, which I shall call *associative* learning, and one that does not, which I shall call *predictive* learning. Moreover, I shall also propose that each type involves different physiological processes.

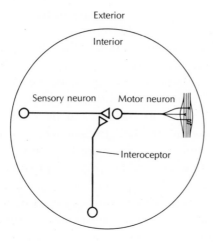

FIGURE 4

homeostasis of the body, it is difficult to conceive how a purely exteroceptive nervous system would be capable of internalizing the "reinforcing properties" of external events. For that to occur, an interoceptive system is required (Figure 4).

The brain's adaptive function lies in its coordination of external and internal motions of the body, thereby sustaining homeostasis. Therefore, initially in evolution the reinforcing value of external events must have been those effects on the body that were transmitted to the brain.

In a diadic nervous system consisting exclusively of exteroceptive and motor neurons we can picture the evolution of different reflexes serving different functions by means of random progressive mutations that altered the connections between nerve cells. Those reflexes that proved to have survival value for the body were selected, whereas those that did not were eliminated. However, once a certain reflex was selected, its mode of action would remain constant without any modulating influences from within the organism. As we saw earlier, a particular reflex can alter with experience only in its vigor but not its selective sensitivity to a particular sensory stimulus. An additional neural element is needed for reflexes to be elicited by novel stimuli encountered with experience, as in animals having the faculty of learning. Perhaps this element is the interoceptive neuron. The interoceptive neuron can be thought of as a "body feeler," sensing whether the state of the body is moving toward or away from homeostasis. If environmental events are positively reinforcing (toward homeostasis) then the interoceptive neuron will effect central neural changes such that patterns of neural activity associated with behavior that preceded the movement toward homeostasis will be generated in the future. If events are negatively reinforcing (away from homeostasis) but the animal executes an effective escape behavior that arrests (or reverses) the decline from homeostasis, then the interoceptive neuron will act to produce central neural alterations that generate behaviors in the future similar to those that arrested the decline from homeostasis. With subsequent repetitions of the same negatively reinforcing circumstances, the escape behaviors will occur progressively earlier in time and eventually the decline from homeostasis will be avoided, as long as internal or external cues that signal the impending decline are available to the animal.

This model should apply to all paradigms of learning, including classical and operant conditioning, which actually involve similar neural events and appear to be different only because of the artificial and arbitrary conditions of the research laboratory. First, let us consider the classical conditioning paradigm of Pavlov (1926). This is traditionally expressed in behavioral terms, as in Figure 5 (where UCS is the unconditioned stimulus, UCR the unconditioned response, and CS the conditioned stimulus).

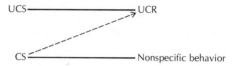

FIGURE 5

This same scheme can be represented as a neural model incorporating an interoceptive neuron, as in Figure 6. Two differences can be noted between these two ᴠrepresentations of classical conditioning. First, in the behavioral model the UCR is depicted as an end effect

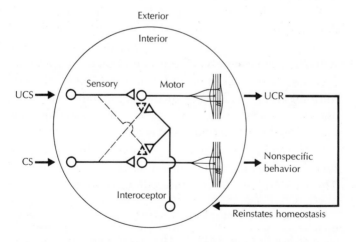

FIGURE 6

having no involvement in the process of establishing
the connection between the CS and·UCR, whereas in
the neural model it feeds back onto the organism so as
to reinstate homeostasis. Second, in the behavioral
model no latent connection is shown between the UCS
and the nonspecific behavior that evolved as a response
to the CS. Moreover, in the behavioral model the
specification of what events constitute the CS and UCS
is decided by the investigator in his experimental
paradigm, rather than being based on the intrinsic potentiality of the animal's nervous system and behavior;
the latter is represented in the neural model. In the
neural model in Figure 6, the initially nonfunctional
synapses (dashed lines) between exteroceptive sensory
and motor neurons become functional if (and only if)
activity in the presynaptic terminals of the sensory
neurons is followed by activity in the terminals of the
interoceptive neurons, which fire whenever the body
approaches homeostasis.

The simplest neural structure capable of learning is
depicted in Figure 7. It would consist of a layer of exteroceptive sensory cells and a layer of motor neurons,
with each sensory cell making a functional synapse with
a certain motor neuron and a nonfunctional synapse
(dashed lines) with each of the other motor neurons;
and of interoceptive neurons whose terminals impinge
upon these nonfunctional synapses.*

This hypothetical neural process of learning conforms to current anatomical and physiological evidence.
The existence of lateral interconnections within indi-

---

*The phenomenon of sensitization (and thus dishabituation) could
even be incorporated into the model without further modification if
we postulate that activity in the presynaptic terminals of nonfunctional synapses increases the efficacy of functional synapses between
other sensory neurons and the same motor neurons.

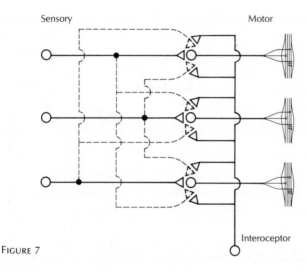

Sensory

Motor

Interoceptor

FIGURE 7

vidual sensory systems of vertebrates, such as the frog, rabbit, cat, and monkey, has been well established.* Sensitization, reflecting interfacilitation between sensory systems, has been demonstrated in the sea hare *Aplysia* (Carew, Castellucci, and Kandel, 1971) and in the spinal cord of the cat (Thompson and Spencer, 1966). Although individual neurons in the primary sensory cortex of mammals are most sensitive to stimulation of a particular sensory modality, they also respond to stimuli of other modalities. In complex nervous systems the sensory cortex could, therefore, represent a locus for the nonfunctional synapses outlined above. Although in Figures 6 and 7 exteroceptive sensory neurons are depicted as synapsing directly onto motor neurons, the same functional scheme could be maintained in more complex nervous systems, with inter-

---

*It should be acknowledged, though, that the lateral interconnections demonstrated so far are almost exclusively inhibitory in their action.

neurons occurring between sensory and motor neurons
and nonfunctional synapses existing between the interneurons and the motor neurons, as depicted in Figure 8.

Sensory   Interneuron   Motor

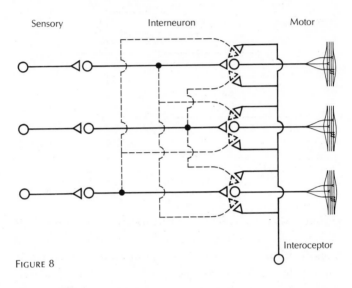

FIGURE 8

Interoceptor

Although I have proposed that interoceptive neurons represent a critical step in the evolution of
learning, might not nonfunctional synapses be made
functional directly by extracellular chemical changes
that represent a movement towards homeostasis? This
is indeed a likely possibility, since in simple animals
the cell bodies of motor neurons are usually located
centrally in the organism. Even in more complex animals nonfunctional synapses in the brain could be made
functional by the actions of hormones in the body. The
notion of interoception should therefore be taken as
broadly as possible so as to include evolutionary developments by which nonfunctional synapses could be
made functional by a change in their chemical *milieu.*

An advantage of a neuronal over a hormonal interoceptive process is the greater speed with which the signals for change toward bodily homeostasis would be transmitted to the brain. It takes longer for the blood to reach the brain from, say, the stomach than for an action potential to reach the brain from a chemically sensitive interoceptive neuron in the stomach.

With our model of learning in mind, let us return for the moment to the phenomenon of habituation. The term "habituation" is normally applied to a decrement in response of innate reflexes to repetitive stimulation. As already discussed, specific reflexes may be regarded as having evolved by virtue of their effectiveness in maintaining homeostasis. That is, under natural conditions unconditioned reflexes tend to be reinforced. Perhaps the phenomenon of habituation observed in the laboratory depends upon the withholding of reinforcement and consequently the absence of arrest or reversal of decline in homeostasis. In that case the efficacy of unconditioned reflexes may be maintained by the same kind of interoceptive feedback as that which induces conditioned reflexes. If this is so, it is clear that extinction and spontaneous recovery of learned behavior depend upon the same neural processes as those involved in the habituation and spontaneous recovery of unconditioned reflexes.

However, habituation and extinction differ in one important respect. Unconditioned reflexes always reappear no matter how often they are habituated, whereas learned behaviors can be completely eliminated with training. The total disappearance of learned behavior can be accounted for by its being superseded by new behaviors that prove to be more effective in reversing or arresting declines from homeostasis. Dur-

ing experimental extinction of a previously learned behavior the energy expended in the now ineffective behavior increases the rate of decline in homeostasis, so
that during the training the animal may learn to remain
motionless or may even fall asleep if no other behavior
proves to be more adaptive in retarding the decline
from homeostasis. Thus, extinction of a learned behavior represents the emergent prepotency of another
behavior or nonbehavior (i.e., remaining motionless).

The organism always acts so as to maintain its bodily state as close to homeostasis as possible, either
by adopting new behaviors that reverse declines from
homeostasis, or by desisting from behaviors that increase the rate of decline from homeostasis. Thus,
energy conservation may be a principal factor when behavior proves to be dysfunctional, so that elimination of
a behavior may be highly adaptive in certain situations.
As has already been discussed, sleep, hibernation, and
torpor are genetically enforced inactive states that serve
to conserve energy and are synchronized with environmental conditions that limit the usefulness of active behavior. Extinction may also be a particular form
of energy conservation.

Forgetting need not be dependent upon any change
specific to the model just described, but might reflect a
property common to all neural pathways, namely, de-
gradation of efficacy with disuse. That is, if a pathway is
not activated over a long period after it has become
functional as a result of learning, then it will eventually
revert back to its initial nonfunctional condition. However, a kind of anamnestic condition could exist in the
pathway such that relearning might be more rapid as a
result of the earlier use of the pathway.

Regardless of the actual processes by which reinforcement is effected in the nervous system, logic
demands that, in the first instance in evolution, differentiation between events that were reinforcing or nonreinforcing had to depend upon the effects of those
events on the body. The nervous system could in no
way predict *a priori* what adaptive value certain events
would have for survival until those events had become
transduced through the body. Unconditioned reflexes
would be perpetuated from one generation to the next
in evolution as a result of their adaptive significance in
sustaining homeostasis. The same considerations must
also apply to the capacity for behavioral plasticity,
which must have depended upon the evolution of those
particular properties of the brain that underlie learning.
Although the neurophysiological model of learning just
presented is almost certainly incorrect in its details, it
has the redeeming virtue of reflecting this underlying
evolutionary principle.

According to the model, the only distinction between
the nervous system of an animal capable of learning and
that of an animal with fixed behavior is the existence of
nonfunctional pathways in the former. In a certain
sense nothing is acquired from the environment and
"added" to the brain that was not there before. New
connections are not established as a result of experience. Instead, latent connections are activated by interaction with the environment. In this way the model
conforms to Plato's view of learning, that we do not
really learn anything new but only "remember" preexistent Forms. Jung's concept of the Collective Unconscious reiterates the same essential idea, since it
implies an innate organic basis for the emergence of

certain behaviors (or psychological events) that are universal but manifested individually (or culturally) in a variety of symbolic forms.

If every sensory neuron were connected with every motor neuron, not only would the number of nonfunctional synapses exceed the number of connections estimated to actually exist in a typical mammalian brain, but this arrangement also would not correspond to the neuroanatomical fact that neural tracts from specific sensory areas impinge upon specific motor areas of the brain. Furthermore, behavioral experimentation has shown that animals do not learn to associate different sensory events with a particular reinforced behavior with equal facility. For instance, Garcia and Koelling (1966) demonstrated that rats learn to associate instances of nausea more readily with a prior experience of an unusual taste ("bait-shy" behavior) than with visual or auditory cues. Seligman (1970) has pointed out that each species exhibits a "preparedness" to learn certain associations more easily than others, reflecting their phylogenetic history.

If the number of latent pathways between sensory and motor neurons were limited in the present model, then an animal would be capable of learning only those sensory-motor associations. Thus the specificity of learning in different species could be accounted for. Only those latent interconnections that had survival value for a species would be passed on from one generation to the next.

But the question might be raised as to why latent interconnections should be needed at all. Why not simply increase the number of functional interconnections and thereby the total number of innate unconditioned reflexes? The answer is that not only would this be

energetically wasteful, since most of the elicited behaviors would not be reinforced, but it would also be
physically impossible because without the capacity of
central coordination many incompatible responses
might be simultaneously activated by a single stimulus.
Clearly, an organism can only do one thing at a time.
Therefore, the excitability of different sensory-motor
pathways must be contingent, so that flexibility in responses can occur under changing circumstances but
with only a single prepotent response being emitted in
any given situation. Only those stimuli that almost invariably lead to reinforcement activate innately functional sensory-motor connections, whereas those that
lead to reinforcement only under certain circumstances
are latently programmed within the nervous system so
as to become effective only when those particular circumstances are repeatedly encountered. Of course,
animals with extremely rigid patterns of behavior can
survive in ecological niches in which conditions have
remained stable over long periods of time. But in variable environments only animals with learning capabilities can survive.

The neural model presented here simplifies learning
theory by dissolving the distinction between classical and operant conditioning, which rests on arbitrary
differences in methodological procedures adopted in
laboratory investigations rather than on any actual differences in organic functions to be found within the
animal itself. In operant conditioning the behavior to be
conditioned is not elicited by the experimenter as it is
in classical conditioning; instead the experimenter
waits for the emergence of the behavior and then presents the reinforcement. With repeated presentations of
"reinforcers" the probability of the behavior being

emitted in the context of the experimental situation increases. At the conclusion of training the behavior occurs either whenever the animal is placed in the experimental environment (which constitutes a conditional stimulus as a whole) or whenever a particular event occurs that the experimenter chooses to isolate as a specific conditional stimulus.

In the neural model presented here operant conditioning makes functional certain latent connections between sensory tracts activated by the conditional stimulus and motor tracts. The motor tracts are activated by preexisting functional connections, which leads to reinforcement. Shortly after reinforcement occurs, interoceptive neurons terminating on the latent connections become active when they sense a movement toward homeostasis. As a result, the latent connections eventually become functionally active and evoke the same motor activities previously evoked by the preexistent functional connections.

In classical conditioning essentially the same neural process occurs, except that the experimenter does not wait for preexistent functional connections onto the motor tracts underlying the particular behavior that he has chosen to reinforce to become spontaneously active. Instead, he directly activates these connections by presentation of a particular UCS. The evoked motor activity results in reinforcement and consequent activation of interoceptive neurons, which in turn bring into operation the latent connections between the sensory tracts activated by the CS and the motor tracts initially activated by the UCS. Thus, classical and operant conditioning differ only in the manner of interaction between experimenter and subject and not in the internal processes, which are essentially the same for each type of learning.

Skinnerians have acknowledged the possibility that the operants they select for conditioning could very well occur as unconditioned responses to UCSs originating from *within* the body. In the classical conditioning paradigm the behavior to be conditioned is elicited by the presentation of a known (external) UCS. In the operant conditioning paradigm the experimenter waits for the "spontaneous" occurrence of the behavior, which in actuality could have been elicited by unidentified internal (or even external) UCSs, or by CSs established earlier but unknown to the experimenter. The range of behaviors that can be shaped and conditioned by operant procedures is limited only by the patience of the experimenter, whereas those that can be classically conditioned are limited by the number of inherited unconditioned reflexes a particular animal possesses.

From this perspective, the difficulty of conditioning autonomic activity (dissociated from skeletal activity) by operant techniques is understandable. Autonomic activity rarely occurs in isolation from ongoing skeletal behavior in the operant conditioning situation, whereas it can be elicited in relative isolation from skeletal behavior by the presentation of suitable unconditioned stimuli, especially by direct electrical stimulation of certain autonomic nerves.

Let us now look more closely at the interoceptive system that detects homeostasis. As I have already argued, a neural system must receive information relating to homeostasis in some direct way from the body itself. It is conceivable that in the first instance in evolution this information pathway was the bloodstream. The most primitive form of learned behavior was probably directed toward the detection and consumption of nutrients, since nutrition is most likely the strongest variable in the "struggle for existence." Procreative functions could be (and are to a great extent in complex organisms) maintained entirely by innate reflexes. A third, most important factor in survival, avoidance or defense from predators, would be nonexistent at the simplest level of animal life (where the high level of egg production obviates its need), reflexive at an intermediate level, and learned at more complex levels. Therefore it seems reasonable to assume that foraging was one of the first behaviors in the course of evolution to involve learning. If this is true, reinforcement must have involved some kind of interoceptive process by which the beneficial effects of ingested nutrients in reversing homeostatic decline could be detected. Excitation of a specialized chemoreceptor by humoral changes following ingestion of food might be the most likely candidate for this process. But, alternatively, the humoral alterations might manifest themselves to the nervous system through the medium of another kind of physiological parameter, such as a change in blood pressure.

Comparative study of behavioral plasticity in simple organisms has not been extensive in the past, but is currently on the rise. Recent work in this area, together with Jennings' (1923) classic review of the behavior of "lower organisms," indicates that associative learning has been *unequivocally* demonstrated only in multicellular organisms, and more particularly, only in those multicellular organisms that possess a closed circulatory system involving a heart.* Of course, this correlation

---

*The claim has been made that classical conditioning has been demonstrated in the flatworm *Planaria*, which lacks a heart (e.g., Corning and Kelley, 1973). However, this claim remains controversial since it has not been confirmed in all investigations where appropriate methodological control procedures for sensitization, backward conditioning, etc., were employed.

may be entirely spurious, but I wish to consider other evidence that indicates that the heart may be a prototypic source of reinforcement, and hence of learning.*

The capacity for learning has been firmly established in mollusks and insects, all of which possess hearts and circulatory systems. Moreover, striking changes in both rate and variability of heartbeat in response to tactile, chemical, and thermal stimuli have been observed in crayfish, lobsters, and snails. Marked changes in heart rate also accompany eating in crayfish (Larimer and Tindel, 1966). These changes are labile and brief in duration. Therefore, it is unlikely that they reflect the energy demands of sustained muscular contraction involved in the movement of the skeleton or the digestive

---

*It would be ironic if the historical identification of the heart as the site of the soul and feeling should be supported by empirical research, since the prevailing viewpoint following Descartes has been that the brain is the source of thought and feeling. D. H. Lawrence took exception to this view, expressing the more ancient belief:

> Man is a creature that still thinks with his blood: "the heart, dwelling in the sea of blood that runs in opposite directions, where chiefly is what men call thought; for the blood round the heart is the thought of men"—And maybe this is true. Maybe all basic thought takes place in the blood around the heart, and is only transferred to the brain. [Apocalypse, London: Martin Secker, 1932, p. 190]

Shortly before this book went to press, I came across the following passage by Norbert Wiener:

> The rapidity with which the conditioned reflex responds to its stimulus is not necessarily an index that the conditioning of the reflex is a process of comparable speed. Thus it seems to me appropriate for a message causing such a conditioning to be carried by the slow but pervasive influence of the blood stream.
> . . . That the blood carries in it substances which may alter nervous action directly or indirectly seems to me very likely, and to be suggested by the actions of some at least of the hormones or internal secretions. [The Human Use of Human Beings, New York: Avon, 1967, p. 99]

system. Instead could it not be that these changes represent processes of reinforcement?

Changes in blood flow, pressure, or chemistry are all potential activators of latent neural pathways. Obviously, it would constitute pure conjecture to attempt to decide among these alternatives in the absence of appropriate experimentation. As mentioned earlier, any one of several factors could operate directly at the nonfunctional synaptic junctions without requiring intermediary interoceptive neurons, even in large animals. But in a massive body, if humoral factors were involved, the transmission time from body to brain would be long. By contrast, alterations in blood pressure are rapidly registered in the brain, with the additional advantage of being able to act on the brain as a whole, in contrast to a neural pathway, which almost certainly would terminate at specific loci in the brain.

If, however, information concerning the state of homeostasis is conveyed to the brain by interoceptive neurons, then deafferentation of the autonomic nervous system should adversely affect the ability of an animal to learn. In one experiment, total autonomic deafferentation of dogs markedly affected their learning ability but did not abolish it (Wynne and Solomon, 1955). However, as I shall argue later, evolutionary changes in neural processes subsequent to those outlined above for the earliest organisms in which learning first appeared are likely to have occurred. In such highly developed animals as dogs, certain types of reinforcing events might be registered directly by the brain, without requiring mediation via the autonomic nervous system.

The hypothesis that autonomic activation, especially of the heart, is associated with reinforcement is consistent with empirical data. Thirsty rats exhibit phasic increases in heart rate when drinking, in contrast to rats who have had free access to water (Eisman, 1966). The same phenomenon is present in humans, who display increased heart rates on eating when they are hungry but not on eating when they feel satiated. Also striking are the significant increases in heart rate produced by direct electrical stimulation of those brain areas that can be used as positive reinforcement in animal training (Sheer, 1961). In fact, electrical stimulation of all those areas of the hypothalamus that have been implicated in processes underlying motivational and emotional behavior evoke dramatic increases in heart rate.

The influence of emotional factors on learning has long been realized but poorly understood. Oddly enough, the efficiency of learning can be increased when positive reinforcement is combined with negative reinforcement, as opposed to the presentation of positive reinforcements alone. Thus, hungry rats will make fewer errors when learning T-mazes if they are electrically shocked whenever they traverse the correct alley leading to the goal box and then eat than if they are allowed to approach the food undisturbed (Muezinger, 1934). A similar effect has been described in studies of animal imprinting. Kovach and Hess (1963) found that neonatal chicks imprinted on a blue ball followed the ball over longer distances if shock was administered when they first observed the ball. These seemingly paradoxical results appear less so in the context of the present model of learning, in which autonomic activation is associated with reinforcement.

At the level of human experience we readily recognize the involvement of emotion in our memories. We have only to reflect for a moment upon our childhood and a flood of memories engulfs us, each one usually marked with a distinct quality of emotional feeling. The power of a great writer such as Proust is his ability to depict his own emotional experiences so vividly that they evoke an empathetic emotional state within ourselves. Proust achieved this not so much by describing his own emotions directly as by portraying events and their relations to earlier experiences in such a way as to evoke those same emotions within us. He was able to do so because we share the same kinds of memories as he had. Freud was greatly concerned with the pervasive effects of emotional experiences from childhood on adult consciousness and behavior. In fact, his work was almost entirely involved with processes of memory. Despite the tremendous impact of his work on psychological thought, standard textbooks in psychology do not regard emotion as an important aspect of the complex process that has come to be called learning and memory. Instead, emotion is either treated as a virtually self-contained concept or it is linked with "motivation."* The attraction of the gross, of the bizarre, of violence, and of direct physical stimulation bordering on that which provokes nausea or fear as provided by horror stories, films, and funfairs—all of which are accompanied by high levels of autonomic arousal—certainly requires explanation, and will be dealt with at greater length in the following chapter.

---

*Most of the experimental work in the area of emotion, even when linked with motivation, has been devoted to negative emotions— anger and fear. There have been few on love and happiness. Those that have been carried out in the area of positive emotions are usually classified under the headings of "sexual behavior" and the analysis of the mental experiences accompanying these is left to the domain of psychoanalysis. The recent behavioral and physiological investigations of sex by Masters and Johnson (1966) represent a departure from this trend and may help to dispel many of the prejudices existing in this field.

Perhaps some of the empirical data I have presented above may lend some credence to the possibility that the mediation of reinforcement is bound up with certain physiological changes that have come to be regarded as emotional. Other data could be added, however my aim is not to be exhaustive in the analysis of every aspect of the neural model of learning presented here, but merely to indicate potential avenues of exploration that may possibly prove more fruitful than those that are currently being pursued.

I have tried to develop a model of learning in which a complex central nervous system could have conceivably evolved from a simple nervous system capable of only a concatenation of fixed reflexes. My emphasis has been on the evolution of a process by which the effects of certain external events on internal bodily states could be conveyed to and affect the central nervous system, so that the probability of a behavior immediately preceding these events in the future would either be increased or decreased, depending upon whether the events were homeostatically reinforcing or nonreinforcing, respectively. Since the determination of reinforcement rests on whether the internal bodily changes move in a direction closer to or away from homeostasis, it finally rests on the question of exactly what physiological parameters, and of what magnitude, constitute homeostasis.

Perhaps an answer to this question may be found by referring back to some of the bioenergetic considerations that I raised earlier. A behavior can be considered adaptive if the number of offspring of that species living to reproductive maturity increases or becomes more stable as a result of the behavior's evolution. Homeostasis can be defined as the matrix of internal bodily conditions necessary for the survival of the species. Although this definition does not allow us to predict whether emergent behaviors (which can evolve as a result of either mutations or learning) will be adaptive, it does allow us to develop a theoretical framework within which to place all species-specific behaviors. Physiological studies, in turn, should allow us to establish the magnitudes of internal parameters that are associated with those same behaviors. In other words, through phylogenetic studies it should be theoretically possible to produce a physiological physiognomy of homeostasis for each individual species. Even if we are successful, however, we shall still remain unable to predict which emerging behaviors might prove adaptive, since we cannot envisage their eventual effects on homeostasis. We must therefore reconcile ourselves, as Heisenberg (1958) did, to the fact that the life sciences must rely on historical factors in their explanations.

The objection might be made that it was just this historical limitation that I so roundly criticized in behaviorism, and which is in no way circumvented by the system offered here. This is indeed the case, but the weakness of historicism is exacerbated in behavioristic analysis by the absence of any general principle concerning the nature of reinforcement, upon which the system so heavily depends. The retort could be made that my approach represents no improvement, since it merely hides the inability to define a principle of reinforcement under the metaphysical concept of "homeostasis." However, the effects of external events on the internal physiology of an organism can be directly observed and formalized in a coherent system, in contrast to the listing of stimulus events and responses that have little significance individually (and whose significance must be derived from inferred events in the body).

In adopting a conception of reinforcement related to homeostasis, the question immediately presents itself of why individual behavioral acts do not occur continuously. If positive reinforcement constitutes reversal of declines in homeostasis, then since metabolism is continuous should not appropriate reflexive or learned behaviors be emitted continuously to sustain homeostasis? That is, would not motivation be continuous, increasing in strength with decline from homeostasis? The fact is that an animal cannot do everything—eating, drinking, mating, protecting, etc.—continuously and therefore simultaneously. Even if it had the behavioral capability and necessary energy to do so, physiological and environmental circumstances normally provide reinforcements only during certain cyclically recurrent periods, as in the daytime for diurnal animals. That is, the occurrence of eating, drinking, and sexual behaviors is *dependent* upon cyclic changes internally (in physiology) and externally (of reinforcers). Behavior is not emitted automatically whenever a certain internal physiological parameter attains a critical level. Instead, the reinforcing consequences of behavioral acts appear to depend upon the degree to which they tend to perpetuate inherited physiological rhythms.

Any behavior that tends to maintain rhythm in a specific physiological variable by bringing about conditions in the future (the dashed wave after time t_0 in Figure 9) is reinforced. Once a certain rhythm has been

Physiological parameter

Time ⟶ t_0

FIGURE 9

established for a physiological variable, that rhythm will be perpetuated provided that the maintenance of the rhythm is not in conflict with another physiological variable. To avoid such conflict, physiological rhythms have different frequencies, are typically out of phase with one another, and are interdependent, so that any alteration of one brings about alterations of others. The phase differences between the internal physiological rhythms is reflected in a corresponding cyclic pattern of behavioral acts that bring about reinforcement and thereby sustain the physiological rhythms themselves.

By holding such a cyclic schema of physiology and behavior in mind, it should prove possible to make reasonable predictions from one moment to the next concerning the potential reinforcing strength of external events. The behavioristic approach to learning does not concern itself with temporal relations between strength of reinforcement and internal physiological parameters. Moreover, it is incapable of predicting which potential reinforcement will predominate over another when several are presented to an animal simultaneously. The isolation of single "drives" for experimental analysis in the laboratory does not resemble natural conditions, in which several "drives" are likely to be simultaneously present at any moment. Investigations along the lines suggested here should yield a cyclic hierarchy of internal physiological rhythms on which a cyclic hierarchy of overt behaviors can be established. Clearly, I have not specified the complex of physiological parameters that must be measured in order to define homeostasis for any given species. This will not be possible until we have determined the normal characteristics of individual physiological rhythms and their relation to the reinforcing strengths of various environmental events.

A neural model of how this cyclic hierarchy of

physiological rhythms is expressed in behavior needs to be established. To do so, let us initially consider the organism as a circadian oscillator of innate activity–inactivity rhythms that become entrained by external geophysical influences. Whenever the organism enters the phase of activity, its activity becomes end-directed in a sequence that reflects the intrinsic hierarchy of the physiological parameters constituting homeostasis. Each particular physiological parameter related to a need—such as glucose concentration for hunger, osmotic pressure for thirst, and androgen concentration for sex—can be represented as a cyclic process embedded within the circadian activity–inactivity oscillator portrayed in Figure 10. This process re-

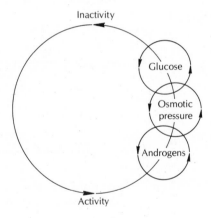

FIGURE 10

quires another set of interoceptive neurons activated by *declines* from homeostasis (as opposed to the set described earlier that register movement toward homeostasis). The set that register declines can be thought of as *motivational* interoceptors; those that register ascents can be thought of as *reinforcement* interoceptors.

As any given parameter declines from homeostasis,
the motivational interoceptors activate specific motor
systems that, innately or by learning, direct behavior so
as to reverse the decline, which constitutes reinforcement. The particular behaviors that emerge will depend
upon the levels of the physiological parameters relative
to one another at any given moment and the history of
reinforcement. To complete the system, therefore, we
need to add the behaviors themselves, the interoceptive
pathways that register the state of each parameter, and
the mutually inhibitory connections between motor
tracts (Figure 11).* Alternatively, mutually inhibitory

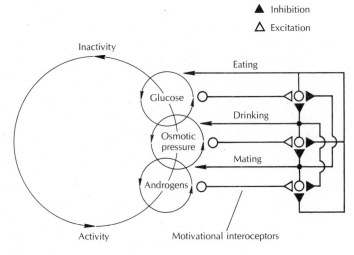

FIGURE 11

*It should be noted that the model of reinforcement and learning
depicted in Figure 7 has not been represented in the model of hierar-
chical behaviors in Figure 11. This omission is purely for the sake of
clarity in presentation, and is not due to any incompatibility between
the two models. The learning model of Figure 7 can be incorporated
into Figure 11 within the loops representing each physiological variable.

connections could exist between different motivational interoceptive systems instead of between motor tracts.

In this simplified scheme the particular need-related behavior present at any moment depends upon the levels of physiological parameters relative to one another. Reflexes that are invariant in strength with time, such as the righting reflex to passive inversion of the body, can easily be incorporated in this model. These reflexes may be prepotent over periodic behaviors and can be introduced into the model by suitable inhibitory connections onto the motor systems governing periodic behaviors. In this way an hierarchy of reflexive and learned behaviors is manifest, with most behaviors exhibiting a constant position within a cyclic hierarchy, whereas others change their position in the hierarchy with time, depending upon their history of reinforcement. Still other behaviors are noncyclic. The integration of the different homeostatic physiological components into a single nervous structure generates a rhythmic pattern of behaviors like the hypothetical (and greatly simplified) pattern in Figure 12.

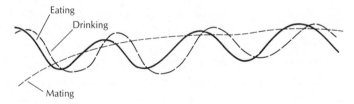

FIGURE 12

The system must have sufficient temporal resolution such that the low point in the rhythm of any particular homeostatic variable should not exactly correspond with that of another variable, otherwise equal and opposite inhibition of the two related behaviors would

result. With appropriate inhibitory connections between the different neural tracts serving each behavioral function, a regular cyclic pattern of behavior is
generated.

The model here should suffice for very small organisms, in which effective behavior rapidly reinstates
homeostasis. For example, a decline in a nutrient in
the blood in very small animals is rapidly reversed by
eating. In larger animals, on the other hand, digestion
takes a considerable amount of time. Because of this
delay, large animals would overeat and eventually become obese if termination of eating depended upon the
actual return to homeostasis. There is evidence for the
existence of rapid interoceptive processes, which I shall
call short-term interoceptors, that register an intake of
food sufficient to return the animal to homeostasis prior
to the actual reversion to homeostasis. In the rat this
appears to be a chemoreceptor in the upper region of
the stomach (Puerto *et al.*, 1976). Eating is triggered in
the rat by activation of the lateral hypothalamus in response to a decline in blood glucose. The short-term
interoceptor is a nutrient-sensitive chemoreceptor in
the stomach that effectively activates the ventromedial
hypothalamus, which in turn inhibits the lateral
hypothalamus so that eating ceases.

In accordance with this model, direct electrical
stimulation of the lateral hypothalamus elicits eating;
surgical lesioning of the ventromedial hypothalamus
produces overeating, such that the lesioned rats eat for
longer durations, take in more food, and thereby become obese. In effect these lesions prevent the lateral
hypothalamus from being influenced by the short-term
interoceptors and thus creates an animal that behaves
like a simple homeostat. The existence of short-term

interoceptors in relatively large organisms implies that
at least some neural modifications were coordinated
with the evolution of increased body size.

Do the short-term interoceptors have reinforcing
properties in themselves or do they merely act as regu-
latory devices, switching off behaviors that presently
lead to reversion to homeostasis and, thereby, to reinforcement? Certain empirical findings, such as the fact
that rats will learn tasks in order to drink saccharin solu-
tions, even though saccharin has no nutritional value, or
that male rats will engage in repetitive sexual intromission without ejaculation, indicates that ingestion of saccharin and sexual intromission are reinforcing even
though they do not apparently affect homeostasis.
Therefore, it appears that activity in short-term interoceptors, such as gastric interoceptors presumably
responsive to saccharin or exteroceptive neurons innervating the penis, can produce reinforcement. By what
evolutionary modifications of the previously developed
neural model could such reinforcing activities come
about?

In the present model reinforcement is signaled by
separate interoceptive pathways for each homeostatic
variable. However, the pathway for the action of reinforcement at the latent connections in the brain need
not be separate for each physiological variable. Appropriate mutations during the course of evolution may
have led to a general neural pathway that effects reinforcement at the latent connections and which is activated by different short-term receptors, each related to a
particular homeostatic variable. I have already cited
evidence indicating that autonomic activation, especially activation of the heart, may underlie reinforcement. If this is so, then it is easy to imagine how the

various homeostatically related short-term interoceptors could evolve so as to impinge upon a cardiac "control center" in the brain. When activated, this center would effect reinforcement by means of some change in a diffuse physiological variable, such as blood pressure or even the electrocardiographic (EKG) wave itself, which sweeps through the entire body and brain. In this way, short-term interoceptors would terminate at one particular locus in the brain, and would not be required to divide into diffuse branches so as to terminate at separate sites in the brain.

In neuroanatomical terms, a system involving a general reinforcing process to the entire brain would be much simpler and therefore much more efficient than one where each homeostatically related interoceptor, or short-term receptor, terminated independently in the brain. The obvious neural locus of this cardiac "control center" serving reinforcement would be the hypothalamus—the area in the brain most intimately involved in the maintenance of homeostasis. This modified neural schema is represented in Figure 13.

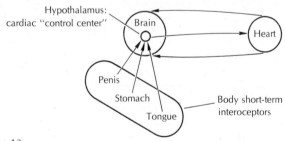

FIGURE 13

It is possible to envisage how, by the normal association of activity in short-term interoceptors with subsequent reversion to homeostasis, mutations resulting

in neural connections between the short-term interoceptors and the hypothalamus could have been
selected.

A neural schema something like that outlined above
could account for the diverse data previously mentioned: of cardiac arhythmia in lobsters and slugs when
touched or during eating; of hypothalamic brain stimulation acting as a reinforcer largely independent of the
homeostatic conditions of the animal; and of electric
shock having reinforcing properties when combined
with natural reinforcers, since electric shock activates
the heart. Hebb (1949) originally suggested that certain
optimal levels of arousal might be reinforcing for behavior. Lindsley (1951) and Stellar (1954) subsequently
developed physiological theories of motivation based
upon concepts of arousal. The above model is consistent with these arousal theories of motivation, since the
continuum of arousal is associated with a continuous
change in the heart rate. Heart rate is lowest during
states of torpor and hibernation, increases during sleep
and wakefulness, and is highest during attentive behavior and vigorous activity.*

The results of a recent self-stimulation experiment by
Ball (1974) are broadly consistent with the above
model. Severing the portion of the vagus nerve innervating the stomach of rats raises the intensity of electrical stimulation of the lateral hypothalamus necessary to
sustain previously acquired levels of lever-pressing

---

*The particular parameters of heart rate associated with the proper-
ties of reinforcement would need to be established, and it is likely
that any absolute level of heart rate is not in itself the critical parameter. It is more likely to be a certain pattern of change in heart rate,
which would account for the reinforcing properties of states of relaxa-
tion and meditation associated with low heart rates, as well as those of
highly arousing experiences associated with high heart rates.

(which activates the current). This result was interpreted by Ball as indicating the presence of a peripheral
source of reinforcement; this possibility had not been
considered by earlier investigators, who considered the
reinforcing properties of electrical brain stimulation to
reside centrally at the site of the electrode.

Since the lesioned rats did continue to stimulate their
own brains, it would have been interesting from the
present point of view to have observed whether subsequent deafferentiation of the portion of the vagus
nerve innervating the heart would have eliminated the
behavior. Sectioning of the vagus nerve from the
stomach could have had the effect of eliminating the
reinforcement provided directly to the brain by the severed portion, or of eliminating a potential influence of
that nerve on the hypothalamus, and thence to the heart
and back to the brain. Although I have emphasized the
potentiality of alterations in heartbeat as a source of
central reinforcement in the brain, nevertheless, one
should be cautious and leave open the possibility of
other autonomic influences, such as gastric activity, also
being potential factors in central reinforcement.

In summary, reinforcement is considered to be tem-
porally dependent upon the inhibitory processes im-
pinging upon any motor network serving a particular
biological function, as well as on the particular state of
the homeostatic variable that a particular behavior subsequently influences. The emergence of neural processes of reinforcement required the evolution of
specialized nerve cells sensitive to the state of the
internal media of the organism, such that they could
"report the state of the system" to the central nervous
system.

I have proposed that in simple nervous systems reinforcement is dependent upon homeostatically related
information arising from within the body. However, the
evolution of more complex nervous systems produced
types of behavior that are characteristic of learning, but
unaccompanied by any events that can be readily perceived as directly affecting homeostasis. These behaviors include latent learning, curiosity, and a great
number of human activities involving symbolism and
often described as "creative." The external events that
are contingent on such activities do not alter body
chemistry, which can be altered only as a result of
internal nervous influences. In the next chapter I shall
try to show how these behaviors nevertheless do set up
contingencies in the future so that other subsequent
behaviors can directly sustain homeostasis.

3 Unfolding

An animal's ability to associate a particular sensory stimulus with certain behaviorally contingent consequences depends upon the animal's capacity to transduce the physical energy of the stimulus into neural activity. Moreover, an examination of the behavioral possibilities afforded by the neural model of learning developed so far will reveal that in any given animal not all sensory stimuli (even though transduced into neural activity) can become associated with behavioral acts. This limitation is due to the animal's "preparedness" to learn only certain associations—those provided for by the "prewired" network of latent neural connections.

However, in higher mammals, and humans in particular, a capacity develops that we call "insight" and "imagination," which allows them to "detach" themselves from the immediate stimulus situation and to symbolize the potential effects of particular acts on the environment. Symbols allow transposition of one sensory modality incapable of influencing motor acts into one that can. For example, a musical score allows one to play a piece that could not be learned by ear. Symbols can also serve a similar function within a single sensory modality. Thus, a map is a representation of visual space greater than can be apprehended in a glance. In addition, humans are able to transcend their innate sensory limitations by inventing technical devices, such as microscopes, X-ray machines, or radar. The development of those learning capabilities that culminate in the use of symbols is the focus of this chapter.

In fixed reflex systems motor activity becomes directed as a result of the combined action of interoceptive activity (related to the state of homeostasis) and exteroceptive activity, which together guide the behavior of the organism in directions that have proved to be adaptive in its phylogeny. In systems with the capability for associative learning behavior is further guided by the effects of individual experience. However, whenever a sequence of habits is ineffective in reversing a decline in homeostasis, increased arousal occurs, and animals often perform novel acts that sometimes prove effective in countering homeostatic decline. If these novel behaviors are successful in reestablishing homeostasis, they become part of the repertory of learned behavior and are emitted under similar circumstances in the future.

But I shall now argue that a further step in evolution took place, whereby novelty, rather than being a means toward immediate homeostatic reinforcement, as in associative learning, became an end in itself, so that

novelty itself became reinforcing. This capability is
identified with what I shall call *predictive* learning, and
is especially characterized by play.

Thus, behavior can be classified into three types,
which reflect three evolutionary modifications in neural
capability: (1) fixed ˜eflex behavior; (2) associative
learning; and (3) predictive learning. The neural model
developed in the previous chapter accounts for behavior in categories 1 and 2. My concern here will be
with the third type of behavior, predictive learning. In
choosing the term "predictive" I do not mean to imply
that this type of learning necessarily involves conscious
anticipation by an animal of the outcome of its own
behavior (although under some circumstances it may do
so). Instead, I wish to develop the idea that in this type
of learning an animal's behavior is more strongly influenced by certain innate structures within its brain than
by environmental contingencies, in contrast to associative learning where the opposite applies.

Variations in behavior can result from variations in
individual life experience without their being considered learned. Each species, taken as a whole, displays
an unfolding sequence of neural potentialities. But the
full range of these potentialities may not be actualized
in every individual animal if the animal fails to encounter the environmental factors that were originally
responsible for their evolution. Because degeneration
occurs in those neural pathways that are not activated,
behavior develops along canalized paths or *creodes*, to
use the term that Waddington (1957) introduced in the
description of the interplay between the environment
and the genes in morphological development.* If an

---

*Waddington's conceptions of embryological development were
subsequently formalized in topological mathematics by Thom (1975).

organism fails to encounter the species-typic environmental factors that the neural potentialities "anticipate," it cannot move easily from one creode to another.
Failure of the neural potentialities to manifest themselves through behavior may threaten the survival of
the organism.

However, variations in behavior can result in exploitation of resources not normally available to the species.
If a variation is the result of genetic mutation, and if it
provides sufficient selective advantage to those individual animals who possess it, it will spread throughout
the population and eventually become the norm. The
change from aberrant to norm may also occur for variations in behavior that are initially unadaptive but which
become adaptive later on because of widespread
changes in the environment.

These considerations lead to the idea of a phylogeny
of behavior, which is the outcome both of changes in
the neurologic network, i.e., the actualization of potential pathways, and changes in the environment (caused
by the behavior patterns) feeding back to the nervous
system. Examination of the ontogenesis of behavior,
and the role of play in particular, should help to clarify
the processes underlying behavioral variation.

The characteristics of play are difficult to define, but
two principal aspects of play are the variability of its
form and its lack of connection with homeostatic reinforcement. Play manifests many characteristics of learning but does not seem to depend upon environmental
events that affect homeostatic variables. It is conceivable that play in animals and humans is merely a manifestation of changing patterns of reflexive activity due
to underlying genetically controlled changes in neural
connections and effectiveness. But the variability in

patterns of play from one individual to another must be regarded as counterevidence to such an interpretation.

If play is in fact learned behavior, then we need to look for the underlying processes of reinforcement that shape the patterns of play. In this search the behavioristic approach to learning and reinforcement does not appear to be fruitful. Conventional reinforcers connected with such natural functions as alimentation, protection, or sexual reproduction do not appear to operate during play. A sequence of such reinforcers in the play of, say, kittens cannot be identified that would be sufficient to account for the acquisition of any particular behavioral aspect, such as pouncing. Similarly, on observing a child quietly engrossed in the task of constructing a tower of bricks, it is inconceivable how such a complex operation could be achieved as a result of schedules of reinforcements, even though schedules of reinforcement are effective in training rats or monkeys to perform complex tasks. Mothers do not coo over their babies every time a sequence of behavior is successfully accomplished. Instead, reinforcement appears to be provided by the mastery of the task itself, so that we must look into the brain of the infant to understand the characteristics of play.

An important aspect of the ontogenesis of the "higher" mammals is the long duration of their postnatal parental care. During this period the infant does not have to depend on its own efforts to satisfy its basic bodily needs, which are normally provided for by one or both parents. The longer the period of infantile care the greater is the potentiality for learning through play. This principle especially distinguishes the primates from other animals. The protection and sustenance provided by an infant's parents frees it for learning, since its initial behavior patterns need be less fixed and can have more "error" or variability than could those of unprotected infants in the wild. Thus, by having the longest infancy of all animals, humans have the greatest learning capabilities. By contrast, precocial mammals, such as the guinea pig, lamb, or goat, have relatively meager learning capacities.

Although adult animals can be shown to be capable of learning in the laboratory by utilization of appropriate schedules of deprivation and reinforcement, when an animal in the wild reaches adulthood it usually learns no more than a few new behaviors, instead leading a somewhat stereotyped existence. It is primarily domesticated animals, being subject to the influence of human beings, that continue to learn during adult life. This is not to say that adult animals are incapable of learning, but rather to place emphasis on infancy as the primary time for learning, so that the length of infancy is related to the ultimate intellectual capacity of an animal.

At one time it was thought that the newborn infant's experience on being born into the world was, as William James described it, one of "blooming, buzzing confusion," and that any constant, organized features of the world had to be learned in order to be perceived. By contrast, Thomas Wolfe in *Look Homeward Angel* depicted himself as a very sophisticated baby who only lacked the key of speech and language to the door of the adult world. The actual state of affairs probably lies somewhere in between these two visions of infancy. Neurophysiological investigations by Hubel and Wiesel (1963) indicate that single neurons in the visual cortex of newborn kittens whose eyes have just opened are selective in their response to visual stimuli. In fact, these neurons do not differ in their feature selectiveness in any marked way from those of adult cats. Similar results indicating that feature detectors are innately present in infant monkeys were recently described by the same authors (Wiesel and Hubel, 1974). These genetically "wired-in" feature detectors selectively respond to straight lines or edges, which may be restricted in length, to a particular angular orientation, or movement in a particular direction.*

Although kittens are born with this innate organization of their nervous system, their ability to detect certain visual features is not retained unless they actually encounter the features in the world during their development. For example, Blakemore (1974) has recently shown that if kittens are reared with their vision restricted to horizontal black-and-white stripes for as brief a period as one hour, then few cells in their visual cortexes will be found that respond to vertical lines.† The importance of this result is that it shows that an inborn potentiality must be actualized in an encounter of those features in the environment originally responsible for its evolution, otherwise that potentiality may be lost, never to be regained in the lifetime of that animal.

---

*More recent studies have not revealed as high a degree of orientation specificity in kittens as originally observed by Hubel and Wiesel (Blakemore and Mitchell, 1973; Pettigrew, 1974). But as Wiesel and Hubel (1974) subsequently pointed out, the visual system of the kitten is relatively immature compared with the monkey, which may explain the greater difficulty in observing orientation specificity in the cortical cells of the kittens.

†There is some question whether this change is to be accounted for by degeneration of innate vertical-detecting neurons or whether the latter change their organization and become horizontal-detecting cells. Current evidence, although it is indirect, tends to favor the latter interpretation (Hirsch and Spinelli, 1971; Blakemore and Cooper, 1970). On the other hand, raising kittens in diffuse nonpatterned light causes degenerative anatomical and physiological changes throughout the visual system (Riesen, 1967).

The same phenomenon has also been observed in imprinting. There exist critical periods during the infancy of birds and mammals when they become attached to the visual or auditory characteristics of their parents. For example, white-crown sparrows acquire their territorial song during infancy on hearing only a few calls of the male parent. They then emit the same song almost a year later when they themselves begin to sing. Infant sparrows that are artificially raised so that they do not hear their species-specific song during the first two months of their life never learn to sing (Marler and Tamura, 1964). Once a critical time span has passed without imprinting of the song having occurred, then imprinting can never occur at a later time. It is worth noting that imprinting is especially characteristic of birds and precocial mammals, who display little or no play.

The process of actualization of an inborn potentiality can be thought of as *phylogenetic reinforcement* of intrinsic neural connections. The nervous system of each species has, by virtue of its evolutionary history, inherited special characteristics that enable it to respond to particular features in the environment. Encountering those features cements those intrinsic neural connections serving that feature-detecting function and thereby constitutes a process of reinforcement. The details of that process still require elaboration. But we can envisage a process similar to that assumed to underlie associative learning, in which latent connections become functional as a result of autonomic activation. More specifically, a neural circuit activated by a particular sensory feature could be innately connected to the autonomic system. When the neural circuit is activated it would produce autonomic activation, which would feed back to the brain and "preserve" the neural connections involved in that circuit. There is little experimental data to support this hypothesis, but the results of the experiments by Kovach and Hess (1963), in which chicks exhibited strong imprinting when given electric shocks simultaneously with their first observation of a visual model, are consistent with this hypothesis. Clearly, the electric shocks must have produced autonomic activation. Alternatively, it is possible that autonomic feedback is unnecessary for the preservation of specific neural circuits and that mere activation of the neural circuits themselves is sufficient to make them functionally stable.

The question might be raised as to whether any active preservation process need be involved in order to understand the phenomena I have just been discussing. Why should not the effects of use and disuse alone be sufficient to explain these losses in behavioral potentiality, since lack of use of neural connections results in their degeneration? In answer to this question, it does seem that something more than mere use and disuse is involved, since adult animals exposed to the same sensory limitations as infants do not exhibit the same degree of behavioral and neural degeneration as do infants.

Given an inherited predisposition for animals to detect certain features in their environments, it is possible that infantile efferent activity is primarily involved in the actualization of afferent activity in innate feature detectors. Since bodily needs are taken care of by the parent(s), motor activity is free to be directed to the "seeking out" of certain patterns of afferent activity.

Reinforcement is not required in the case of the development of innate patterns of efferent activity, since motor activity is dependent upon internal factors only and does not require interaction with the environment; in this case the external world is simply a passive mechanical substrate on which the animal moves. Nerve cells in motor pathways close to muscles can exhibit endogenous rhythmic activity that is not dependent upon sensory influx from external stimuli or from movement-produced feedback. The results of ontogenetic studies of motor development (Hamburger, 1970; Davis, 1973) demonstrate that there are intrinsic patterns of neural activity present in the spinal cord before there are any fully developed functional connections between the spinal cord and the muscles. Even more remarkable is the finding that the patterns of neural activity correspond in many ways to the patterns seen in older animals, in whom the connections between spinal cord and muscles are complete. Even at the gross behavioral level, Berman and Berman (1973) demonstrated that relatively normal patterns of walking and reaching develop in newborn monkeys whose sensory nerves in the forelimbs are severed prior to delivery. Thus, sensory feedback provides the organism with information concerning the effectiveness of its movements but is not necessary for the generation of the movements themselves.

The processes whereby motor neurons make functional connections during development with muscle fibers is not thoroughly understood. But it does appear that motor neurons become functionally differentiated from one another independently of the differentiation of individual muscle fibers, and then link up with muscle fibers in an ordered way, probably by chemotaxic mechanisms.

But although certain patterns of motor activity, such

as crawling, walking, grasping, righting, and flying, do not need to be learned, it does not necessarily follow that other, learned aspects of motor activity cannot be acquired simultaneously during infancy. Therefore, I propose that motor activity that results in the activation of feature detectors is learned, so that phylogenetic reinforcement at the afferent level is associated with ontogenetic reinforcement at the efferent level. This associative process I shall call *predictive* learning.

The phylogenetic and ontogenetic aspects of reinforcement are illustrated by experiments in which kittens (Held and Hein, 1963) and neonatal monkeys (Held and Bauer, 1967) were raised under conditions of restricted movement. Kittens who were passively moved about in a visual environment, and not allowed to walk by themselves, were subsequently unable to walk about without bumping into things, and were also unable to make appropriate anticipatory placing responses of their forelimbs when lowered towards a flat surface. Similarly, monkeys reared so that they were unable to see their hands did not reach for food when it was held in front of them, even though they could move their hands normally. After being allowed total freedom of movement for some time, the kittens and monkeys did eventually learn to walk and run about without colliding with objects and performed appropriate placing and reaching responses with their limbs.

One can conclude from these results that restricted movement did not prevent the phylogenetic reinforcement of the afferent feature-detecting processes. Afferent visual activity was sufficient even in the absence of normal efferent activity to prevent the degeneration of the innate feature-detecting systems. The fact that the experimental animals did not exhibit any marked retardation in their gross movements supports the earlier conclusion that basic patterns of efferent activity mature independently of experience. What was lacking in these animals during their period of restriction was ontogenetic reinforcement of efferent activity, which under normal conditions is responsible for phylogenetic reinforcement. Instead of the normal phylogenetic reinforcement provided by the infants' own activities, the experimenters were responsible for it by moving the infants passively in the environment, so that the motor behavior of the infants did not become coordinated with their visual environment.

Animals raised in total darkness or in uniform nonpatterned light (a *Ganzfeld*) do not receive phylogenetic reinforcement of their feature detectors, which then degenerate, never to be regained. Such animals therefore have no opportunity for ontogenetic reinforcement and although able to locomote normally, because of the normal maturation of efferent processes, never learn to avoid obstacles.

Patterns of limb movement no doubt also reinforce phylogenetic feature detectors in auditory, tactile, and kinesthetic modes in a similar way. Associative learning resulting in homeostatic reinforcement might also take place simultaneously with phylogenetic reinforcement. Thus, adult monkeys whose forelimbs were totally deafferented learned to point to a visual target in front of them for food rewards, even though they could not see their own arms (Taub, Goldberg, and Taub, 1975). The monkeys learned to generate a specific pattern of efferent activity conditionally related to a specific pattern of afferent activity that was followed by a reversal of homeostatic decline. Similar capabilities of associative learning might also be present in early infancy.

Animals with the greatest capabilities for predictive learning through play are relatively immobile at birth, and the movements they do make tend to be irregular and disorganized. However, whenever motor behavior is sufficiently stereotypic the potentiality of establishing efferent–reafferent correlations does exist. The first correlations of this type probably occur between such activities as closing the eyes and the disappearance of light, sucking on the breast and the gushing of milk into the mouth, or swallowing and the sensation of fluid passing to the stomach.

But what about afferent–afferent associations, or what is known as sensory–sensory learning? For example, can an animal learn to associate the flashing of a light with the ringing of a bell in the absence of homeostatic reinforcement and without being required to perform a specific action? Experiments on sensory–sensory learning have yielded inconclusive results. In order to assess whether learning is taking place in an animal or human being other than ourselves, we have to observe an alteration in their overt behavior. But in such experiments afferent activity should not be accompanied by efferent activity, since this might lead to alterations in homeostatic conditions and thus reinforcement of the afferent–afferent associations. Therefore, experimentation in this area has usually involved the temporary paralysis of an animal during the putative acquisition of afferent–afferent associations. Such animal experiments have produced conflicting findings on whether sensory–sensory learning actually occurs or not. However, it should be emphasized that the kinds of stimuli used in these experiments, such as flashes of light or pure auditory tones, are selected for their physical purity, and bear little resemblance to the complex kinds of sensory events, such as the snap of a twig, that an animal typically encounters in nature. Thus, in behavioral experimentation we face the dilemma of having to use stimulus events that can be precisely calibrated and yet wishing to use ones that also bear some resemblance to natural events.

By relying on animal data alone, it might be premature to conclude that afferent–afferent learning does not occur, and for this reason we must turn to human phenomenological data for a tentative answer to this question. In phenomonological terms exactly how would afferent–afferent learning be manifested? Presumably, by the consistent evocation of one image whenever another occurs—essentially, a linking up of images. Does this in fact occur when the sensory stimuli do not directly affect homeostatic variables? If we reflect on our own individual experience it certainly seems that it does. The emergence of the visual image of a flower in response to its scent is one example. Proust, the supreme portrayer of sensory experience, time and again reveals to us the mystery and intrinsic force of sensations that impress themselves in memory, especially during childhood, regardless of any utilitarian value they may have. Take for example this passage from *Remembrance of Things Past.*

> A hawthorn . . . was attired even more richly than the rest, for the flowers which clung to its branches, one above another, so thickly as to leave no part of the tree undecorated, like the tassels wreathed about the crook of a rococo shepherdess were every one of them precisely the colour of some edible and delicious thing, or of some exquisite addition to one's costume for a great festival, which col-

ours, inasmuch as they make plain the reason for their
superiority, are those whose beauty is most evident to the
eyes of children, and for that reason must always seem
more vivid and natural than any other tints, even after the
child's mind has realized that they offer no gratification to
the appetite, and have not been selected by the
dressmaker. And, indeed, I had felt at once, as I had felt
before the white blossom, but now still more marvelling,
that it was in no artifical manner, by no device of human
construction, that the festal intention of these flowers was
revealed, but that it was Nature herself who had spontaneously expressed it (with the simplicity of a woman
from a village shop, labouring at the decoration of a street
altar for some procession) by burying the bush in these
little rosettes almost too ravishing in colour, this rustic
"pompadour." High up in the branches, like so many of
those tiny rose-trees, their pots concealed in jackets of
paper lace, whose slender stems rise in a forest from the
altar on the greater festivals, a thousand buds were swell-
ing and opening, paler in colour, but each disclosing as it
bursts, as at the bottom of a cup of pink marble, its blood-
red stain, and suggesting even more strongly than full-
blown flowers the special, irresistible quality of the
hawthorn-tree, which wherever it budded, wherever it
was about to blossom, could bud and blossom in pink
flowers alone.*

Common to this and other examples of seemingly
pure sensory–sensory association is the evocation of a
strong emotional tone, as in this passage from Proust.

At a bend in the road I experienced, suddenly, that special pleasure, which bore no resemblence to any other,
when I caught sight of the twin steeples of Martinville, on
which the setting sun was playing while the movement of
the carriage and the windings of the road seemed to keep
them continually changing their position; and then of a
third steeple, that of Vieuxvicq, which, although sepa-

---

*Volume I: "Swann's Way," New York: Modern Library, 1934, pp.
106–108.

rated from them by a hill and a valley, and rising from
rather higher ground in the distance, appeared none the
less to be standing by their side. . . .

I did not know the reason for the pleasure which I
found in seeing them upon the horizon, and the business
of trying to find out what that reason was seemed to me
irksome; I wished only to keep in reserve in my brain
those converging lines, moving in the sunshine, and, for
the time being, to think of them no more.*

The question remains whether the emotional feeling
occurs automatically because of the activation of an innate releasing mechanism triggered by certain features,
which results in reinforcement by way of the physiological processes suggested earlier; or whether the emotional tone arises for other reasons, not immediately
connected with the sensations, and which only coinci-
dentally effect the association of the two. Regardless of
the answer to this question, it does seem that the ac-
companiment of sensory–sensory association by emotional feelings indicates that autonomic activation is
involved, reinforcing associations between various
perceptual images. But this process of sensory–sensory
association need not necessarily trigger efferent processes.

But if there is no immediate relationship between
sensory–sensory associations and behavior, what adaptive value could such associations serve? The answer is
that the innate nervous system has an economically fi-
nite number of connections, and this requires the development of a certain redundancy in perception with
experience. If afferent activity in an innate feature-
detecting system of neurons, denoting one feature of a
stimulus is repeatedly accompanied by afferent activity

*"Swann's Way,"p. 138.

denoting another sensory feature not in an innate feature-detecting system, the learned association of the two would allow an animal to detect the stimulus and register its adaptive significance even when the genetically selected feature was absent. Information theory has shown the functional significance of redundancy. In spelling, for example, considerable redundancy exists such that several characters can be absent without loss of comprehension. The natural selection of only one or two primary features of an event for genetically predetermined detection by the brain is highly economic if a process is also provided for the learning of other features of the object by association. This economy therefore constitutes the adaptive value of afferent–afferent learning.

It should be constantly borne in mind that a particular species' perceptual experience has evolved through natural selection from an infinite multitude of possible experiences, so that only those feature detectors that promote survival are preserved. The needless multiplication of genetically prewired feature detectors would create demands on the parents to provide additional protection and nutrients over a longer period in order to permit the additional connections to become established. The building into the neonatal brain of unnecessary redundant feature detectors would reduce the brain's efficiency.

An animal is born with a relatively small number of genetically determined feature detectors. During the animal's development the features associated with these basic detectors link up with other perceptual features, accompanied by emotional arousal, resulting in the build-up of additional detectors corresponding to Konorski's (1967) "gnostic units." This process is essentially a reformulation of Hebb's (1949) original proposition that learning involves the building up with experience of perceptual "cell assemblies."

The involvement of autonomic activation and emotion in the acquisition of sensory–sensory associations during childhood is attested to not only in the writings of novelists, who ground their work in those phenomenal experiences common to humanity, but also in the literature of psychoanalysis. In fact, in psychoanalytic theory the sensory associations acquired during infancy and early childhood are the strongest of all. The fact that our recall of childhood experiences is often more vivid than that of experiences acquired later in life, especially as we grow older, attests to this viewpoint.

During development the brain correlates any combination of afferent and efferent patterns of activity, regardless of whether or not they are of the same type, provided autonomic activation also acts to reinforce the correlation. Autonomic activation can result from a direct reversal of homeostatic decline or can be triggered by perceptual processes that themselves evolved because they were regularly followed in the history of the species by reversal of homeostatic decline. Ultimately, reinforcement is dependent upon the immediate or eventual occurrence of particular patterns of efferent activity that result in the reinstatement of homeostasis.

Let us now return to a further consideration of play and how the model of learning presented here may help us understand the development of novel behaviors that do not immediately affect homeostasis. As proposed above, the activation of feature detectors constitutes phylogenetic reinforcement of afferent processes, whereas the learning of specific behaviors that bring about phylogenetic reinforcement involves ontogenetic reinforcement of patterns of efferent activity. Different activities during play will be reinforced, then, to the

degree that they result in the activation of innate feature
detectors, which are genetically linked with the autonomic system so as to activate it. The system can be
represented as in Figure 14.

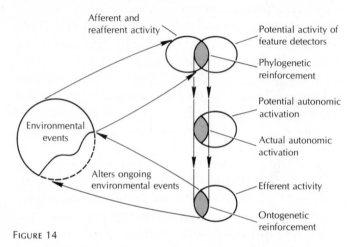

FIGURE 14

Patterns of efferent activity alter ongoing environmental events and feed back to the organism so as to
generate reafferent activity. Autonomic activity results
if the innate feature detectors are activated. Interoceptive feedback from the autonomic system results in
reinforcement of afferent–afferent associations (phylogenetic reinforcement) and reinforcement of efferent
activity (ontogenetic reinforcement). The strength of
reinforcement depends therefore upon the extent to
which the feature detectors are activated.

Since behavior is shaped by internal processes, those
movements that produce greater activation of feature
detectors will cause greater autonomic activation and
reinforcement. In this way species-specific patterns of
motor behavior, such as pursuing and pouncing on a
prey or complex mating postures, are acquired. For

example, a well-executed pounce by a cat would be accompanied by the complete activation of feature detectors selectively responsive to a particular pattern of visual "streaming" (cf. Gibson, 1966). As a kitten develops, each movement in play that partially activates such "streaming" detectors is reinforced, so that successive movements are internally shaped until the complete mature act of pouncing is acquired.

Once each species-specific behavior pattern has been learned it develops no further, remaining fixed until eventually called into use by homeostatically related needs as the animal matures under the appropriate environmental conditions. These acquired behaviors represent the biologically adaptive functions served by the feature detectors. The species-typic adult repertory of behavior need not be genetically programmed into the nervous system as a complex series of prewired efferent networks, only its effects on relatively simple afferent networks. At least in animals other than primates, once all feature detectors have been activated and phylogenetic reinforcement has taken place, play ceases.

Humans represent the greatest exception to this rule and never cease to play until they die.* Pet animals also continue to play in adult life, but domestication is the critical factor—they are subject to the influence of man's own playfulness. The wisdom of *Homo sapiens* is achieved through extension of play throughout his life. The lengthening of infancy allows the learning of more

---

*If play continues into adulthood, and yet we characterize childhood by play, what distinguishes the adult from the child? The distinction lies not in the presence or absence of play, but in the formal adoption of social roles within a culture. Although the onset of sexual maturity is regarded in many cultures as marking the distinction between childhood and adulthood, and is so signified by initiation ceremonies, in technologically advanced cultures it usually occurs considerably earlier than the time at which the person is regarded as "adult."

and more complex behavior and reaches a maximum in humans, who never "grow up" in the sense that play never ceases, since ontogenetic reinforcement never terminates. "The child is father of the man" by virtue of inherited feature detectors, whose potential activities are only rarely totally realized in an individual lifetime.

But what are the psychological correlates of these feature detectors in humans? I think the answer has largely been given to us by Jung. They are the inherited archetypes, which are the structural components of the Collective Unconscious. The connection between archetypes and neural feature detectors is indicated by Jung's synonyms for the archetype—primordial image, imago, mythological image, and behavior pattern. Jung's essential ideas of the archetype have been succinctly described by Hall and Nordby.

> . . . The collective unconscious is a reservoir of latent images, usually called *primordial images* by Jung. *Primordial* means "first" or "original"; therefore a primordial image refers to the earliest development of the psyche. Man inherits these images from his ancestral past, a past that includes all of his human ancestors as well as his prehuman or animal ancestors. These racial images are not inherited in the sense that a person consciously remembers or has images that his ancestors had. Rather they are predispositions or potentialities for experiencing and responding to the world in the same ways that his ancestors did. . . .
>
> The contents of the collective unconscious are called *archetypes*. The word "archetypes" means an original model after which other similar things are patterned. A synonym is *prototype*.
>
> Jung spent much time during the last forty years of his life investigating and writing about the archetypes. Among the numerous archetypes that he identified and described are those of birth, rebirth, death, power, magic,

the hero, the child, the trickster, God, the demon, the wise old man, the earth mother, the giant, many natural objects like trees, the sun, the moon, wind, rivers, fire, and animals, and many man-made objects such as rings and weapons. Jung wrote, "There are as many archetypes as there are typical situations in life. Endless repetition has engraved these experiences into our psychic constitution, not in the forms of images filled with content, but at first only as *forms without content,* representing merely the possibility of a certain type of perception and action. . . . A primordial image is determined as to its content only when it becomes conscious and is therefore filled out with the material of conscious experience". . . .

Archetypes are universal: that is, everyone inherits the same basic archetypal images. Every infant throughout the world inherits a mother archetype. This preformed image of the mother is then developed into a definite image by the actual mother's appearance and behavior and by the relationships and experiences the baby has with her. Individual differences in the expression of the mother archetype soon appear, however, since experiences with mothers and child-rearing practices vary from family to family, and even between one child and another in the same family. Jung does note, however, that when racial differentiation took place, essential differences in the collective unconscious of the various races also appeared.*

Jung (1960a) remarked that people were inclined to view his theory of inherited archetypes as meaning "inherited ideas." He wrote: ". . . there is naturally no question of that. It is rather a question of inherited *possibilities* of ideas, paths which have gradually been traced out through the cumulative experience of our ancestors. To deny the inheritance of these paths would be tantamount to denying the inheritance of the brain.

---

*A *Primer of Jungian Psychology,* New American Library, 1973, pp. 39–43.

To be consistent, such skeptics would have to assert
that the child is born with a brain of an ape. But since it
is born with a human brain, this must sooner or later
begin to function in a human way, and it will necessarily begin at the level of the most recent ancestors."

Certainly, given the sparsity of our present state of
knowledge of the brain, the identification of human feature detectors with Jungian archetypes can be little
more than metaphorical. However, considering the relatively high complexity of visual feature detectors in
cats and even frogs, it should not exceed the bounds of
imagination that such rich constructs as the archetypes
could be embodied in the human brain. Their very
complexity would tend to guarantee the continuance of
"play" throughout life. The high complexity of such feature detectors would allow for activation of portions of
the detector systems in a wide variety of ways under
many different environmental and behavioral circumstances. It would also allow for the development of
what has come to be called "personality." This process
of intellectual growth is linked with Jung's central archetype, the Self—the organizing principle of the personality. The complete activation of this feature (in
neural terms), or self-realization (in phenomenological
terms), involves the drawing together and harmoniza-
tion of all the other archetypes. Jung (1953) concluded
that ". . . the Self is our life's goal, for it is the com-
pletest expression of that fateful combination we call
individuality. . . ." For the few sages and mystics who
achieve this goal, perhaps one can say that their play
has ended.

The process of "self-actualization" to a great extent
involves the progressive activation of certain feature detectors through interaction with the kinds of environ-

ment each person encounters.* At a more complex
level, structural anthropologists, led by Lévi-Strauss,
are delineating how universal structural characteristics
of human thought are transformed into universal structural characteristics of human culture.

Jung stressed that an archetype was a universal
thought form that contains a large element of emotion.
The proposition that activation of feature detectors results in activation of the autonomic system is consistent
with Jung's formulations. We can also see how novel
experience and behavior would be reinforced by the
activation of latent feature detectors. However, in order
to also explain the phenomena of habituation and bore-
dom it appears necessary to postulate the following
corollary principle. Once phylogenetic reinforcement
of portions of feature detectors has occurred, each reac-
tivation of those same portions produces a progressively
decreased activation of the autonomic system. During
development, when a pattern of afferent–reafferent activity first activates a portion of an inherited feature detector, it will also effect phylogenetic reinforcement of
afferent–afferent associations contemporaneous with it,
as well as ontogenetic reinforcement of patterns of
efferent activity that just preceded it. Once this has occurred, "the path has been laid" for reinforcement by
future events.

Whether or not reinforcement of a behavior will be
positive or negative (its sign) and the determination of
its strength will depend upon the relation between the
pattern of afferent–reafferent activity and previously

---

*Contemporary views of self-actualization presented by humanistic
psychologists, such as Maslow (1954), in essence represent a reformulation of ideas originated by Goldstein and Jung.

reinforced patterns, as represented in Figure 15. In this figure the circles A–F represent exemplary patterns of activation in a single feature-detecting system. If a pattern of afferent–reafferent activity completely corresponds with a previously reinforced pattern (A), then it has zero reinforcing properties.* The greater the degree of noncorrespondence, the greater the strength of positive reinforcement—but only up to a certain critical point (B). Beyond this point the strength of positive reinforcement declines, falling back to zero, as at C, where the entire feature detector is activated and the extent of novel activity is at its maximum. If the degree of noncorrespondence is even greater, as in D, components of the feature detector are activated that are discontinuous with those previously reinforced, which results in negative reinforcement. Maximum negative reinforcement occurs when those components previously reinforced are not activated (E). Negative reinforcement decreases with less activity in the feature detector (F). By this process reinforcement is regulated in such a manner that behaviors are gradually shaped toward the mature pattern.

A similar pattern is followed in experiences associated with different patterns of neural activity, so that the strength and polarity of one's feelings—the affective tone—relates to the degree of correspondence between present and past experiences.

Experiences that are identical with earlier experiences are felt to be boring and dull. New experiences that resemble older experiences, but vary from them in

---

*But it should be recognized that this holds true only so long as the behavior does not affect the level of homeostasis, for if it does, then associative learning becomes possible.

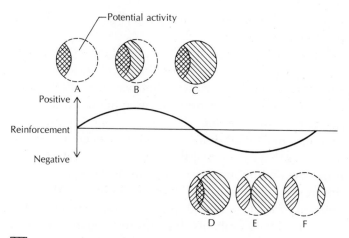

Phylogenetic (previous) reinforcement

Present afferent–reafferent activity

FIGURE 15

unique ways, are felt to be pleasant and also arousing (because of the autonomic activation involved). Novelty will thus be sought for its own sake, but will nevertheless usually bear a definite relation to past experience. However, beyond a certain degree of novelty the degree of pleasantness declines and falls back to zero—it is at this point that the experiences are felt to be strange or bizarre. As the degree of novelty continues to increase, the intensity of negative feeling also increases, so that the experiences become weird, grotesque, horrific, or even terrifying, and are likely to be avoided in the future. As the experiences reach greater and greater degrees of novelty, negative feelings subside and the experiences become irrelevant to anything that has been experienced before; eventually they lose "meaning" and do not evoke any affective response, either positive or negative.

It is probably unnecessary to illustrate the application of this model with many examples. Certainly the pleasure and search for novelty in books, music, films, theater, art, and even nature is commonplace. It is in phenomena such as funfairs and the representation of violence in "entertainment" that one encounters experiences that can elicit either positive or negative feelings, depending upon constitutional or experiential differences between individuals. Funfair rides are enjoyed by some persons but frightening to others. The emotion evoked probably depends to some extent upon the kinds of motion experienced in the past. Horror films can be experienced as pleasantly exciting up to a certain point. As Aristotle remarked: "Objects that in themselves we view with pain, we delight to contemplate when reproduced with minute fidelity: such as the forms of the most ignoble animals and of dead bodies. The cause of this again is that to learn gives the liveliest pleasure. . . ."* But as the events portrayed in the film become more and more macabre or grotesque, they can become unpleasant. If the events become completely divorced from any previously experienced human reality, then they have no affective influence.

Because of the complexity of human feature detectors, novelty continues to occur throughout the individual's life, even though under close examination what often appears to be novel turns out to be merely a variation of an old experience. We create the basis for these variations by fashioning our environment through particular acts that bring certain images into actuality. The

---

*Poetics, in Aristotle's Theory of Poetry and Fine Art, S. H. Butcher, New York: Dover, 1951, p. 15.

images that arise within us constitute what is commonly called fantasy. What factors determine the nature of the particular fantasies that emerge are probably beyond our explanation at present.

The exploitation of play by its extension throughout life represents an example of *pedomorphosis*—a mode of evolution in which the adult form of the descendent resembles the young form of the ancestor. Pedomorphosis is brought about by the same evolutionary process as *neoteny*—the retention of larval characteristics at sexual maturity—in which the development of the reproductive system accelerates relative to that of the rest of the body, so that animals in successive generations become sexually mature earlier in life. Garstang (1928), who introduced the term "pedomorphosis," suggested that it has been one of the most important means of evolutionary change and that it might have been involved in the evolution of the first vertebrates. Thus, the larvae of certain echinoderms, such as sea cucumbers, are mobile and possess ciliated bands (auricularia) whose disposition bears some resemblance to the neurenteric canal of the vertebrate nervous system. This mobility permits the larvae to maintain themselves on surface plankton, and explains the wide distribution of the species. On metamorphosis, this mobility disappears and the animals become sessile bottom-dwellers. Garstang suggested that through pedomorphosis sexual maturity ultimately occurred in the mobile larval state itself, at which point the protovertebrate emerged. It is not unlikely that the evolution of predictive learning, whereby the adaptive value of play is extended into adult life, also represents pedomorphosis.

The adaptive significance of predictive learning lies in its allowing humans to adapt to changes in their physical and social environment. Since the environment of animals tends to be relatively stable (unless it is disturbed by humans), a fixed repertory of behavior that effectively serves them throughout their lives is acquired in an early period of play. If long-term environmental changes do occur, natural selection may favor altered behaviors resulting from random mutations affecting the neural structures of feature detectors. Humans, on the other hand, are able to continually adapt to a changing environment because of the progressive activation of feature detectors brought about by the extension of play throughout life. However, this extension of play has the potential disadvantage of creating a vicious circle in which altered behaviors themselves cause further changes in the environment. Animals are limited in their ability to adapt to sudden changes in the environment by man because of their limited capacity for predictive learning. Hence, the current ecological crisis and its threat to the survival of large numbers of species throughout the world largely results from human technology, which in large measure is the direct result of the instinct for play.

In the few instances in which new "cultural" habits have been observed to evolve in primates, it is interesting that they tend to be initially acquired by young animals and subsequently adopted by adults. Examples of these are potato-washing, wheat-washing, and bathing behaviors by Japanese macaques, which were first observed in juvenile animals (Kawai, 1965).

Predictive learning can be associated with experiential images of future contingencies; these images occur whenever neural feature detectors are activated. Activation might occur when the animal observes another animal displaying a pattern of behavior with a particular feature. There is good evidence of this in song birds. I mentioned earlier how a white-crown sparrow must hear the song of a territorial male adult during the first two months of its life if it is to sing effectively, attract a mate, and defend its own territory the following year. As an infant, therefore, it acquires an auditory image that is associated with a feature detector corresponding to its species-specific territorial song. When it begins to sing the next year, however, it does not immediately burst into a complete adult song, but instead "babbles" for about a week until it eventually learns the complete song. Moreover, birds that have been exposed to adult songs as infants but are subsequently surgically deafened, so that they are unable to hear themselves sing, are unable to learn to sing (Konishi, 1965).

Thus, imitation can be understood through the activation of feature detectors. But difficulty is encountered when imitation is based on visual learning, since the visual image of one's parents performing an action is very different from the visual perceptions experienced when one is performing that action oneself. The ability of primates and especially humans to transform a visual image of observed action into a somatosensory image of a self-produced action depends upon their special ability for employing symbols.

I conclude this chapter with the following quotation from Robert Musil's *The Man Without Qualities.*

> He was in that state of semi-sleep in which the patterns of the imagination begin to race after each other. He saw before him the barrel of a gun, and saw himself looking down into the darkness of it, saw in it a shadowy nothingness, the obscurity that blocked the depths, and felt there was a strange concord and a queer coincidence in the fact that this same image of a loaded gun had in his youth

been a favourite image of his, expressive of his will,
charged as this will had always been with purpose, and
always trained on its target. And all at once he saw, one
after the other, many such pictures as that of the pistol and
that of himself standing together with Tuzzi. There was a
meadow in the early morning. Then, seen from a train,
there was a long, winding river-valley, filled with dense
evening mists. Then, at the far end of Europe, there was a
place where he had parted from the woman he had loved:
the woman's image had gone, but that of the unmetalled
roads and the thatched cottages was as fresh as if it had
been only yesterday. The hair in the arm-pit was all that
was left of another woman he had loved. Shreds of tunes
occurred to him. Someone's characteristic movement. . . .
The smell of flower-beds—unnoticed once while violent
words were spoken over them, words born of the profound emotions in the speakers' souls—now came back to
him, the scent of flowers outliving the forgotten words
and people. A man on various paths, man it was almost
painful to look at: he himself . . . like a row of puppets
abandoned, the springs broken long ago. . . . One would
think such random images were the most transient of
things in the world, but there comes a moment when the
whole life splits up into such images, and they alone
stand along the road of one's life; it is as though this road
led only on from them and back to them again, and
as though destiny did not take its bearings from resolves
and ideas, but from these mysterious, half-meaningless
pictures.*

---

*Volume II, "The Like of It Now Happens II," London: Secker and
Warburg, 1961, p. 452.

Differentiation 4

When an animal is motionless, correlations between patterns of afferent activity represent aspects of the environment independent of the animal. Whenever an animal emits patterns of efferent activity, it produces bodily movement that affects its sensory receptors and thereby "interjects itself" into otherwise purely externally originating patterns of afferent activity. Afferent activity independent of an animal's own actions is associated with the animal's image of the external world. Theoretically, it should be possible to derive a mathematical transformation function that relates patterns of efferent activity to reafferent activity. This function would represent the effect of the behavior on the environment relative to the body. The establishment of certain invariant relations between patterns of efferent and reafferent activity, as in kittens learning to pounce, constitutes what I have called predictive learning. It is a process involving *correlation* between activities in different parts of the brain. I shall now deal with the process of *differentiation*, present at all levels of brain function and fundamental to an understanding of cognition.

Perception depends upon the evolution of different types of primary receptors selective to only certain qualities of physical stimulation. The particular physical characteristics selected depend upon the evolutionary history of each species. Each species evolved with its own particular constellation of specific receptors, selected because of their adaptive value. The phenomenal world of snakes that feed on warm-blooded animals and are capable of sensing infra-red radiation is probably dominated by patches of heat and cold, whereas ours is dominated by patches of different colors and intensities of light. But in each case the phenomenal world arises because of *differential* levels of activation within an array of primary receptors.

If all the nerve cells constituting a perceptual system were to fire at uniform rates, there would be no content to perception. This situation is virtually attained in the visual system in total darkness or with the eyes closed.* The disappearance of perceived forms following artificial stabilization of the visual image on the retina is due to the adaptation of photoreceptors to constant physical stimulation. The early studies by Gelb (1929) indicated that the perception of brightness depends upon differences in relative rates of neural activity in the retina and does not conform to the physical measures

---

*Perceptions of random spots of brightness under these conditions presumably depend upon nonrandom firing of cells caused by influences within the eye and brain.

of brightness obtained with a photometer. The same considerations apply to simultaneous brightness or color-contrast phenomena and after-images, in which perception is dependent on relative rates of activity of nerve cells across boundaries and is not a direct representation of external, physically measurable light intensities. The brain functions as a comparator of relative rates of activity in the peripheral nervous system.

If it were not for the fact that some of the characteristics of after-images are inconsistent with other aspects of external experience, we would certainly regard after-images as genuine parts of external reality. However, the fact that they can be superimposed upon a more vivid and extensive background of visual objects, and made to move relative to this background by moving our eyes, makes us attribute them to internal causes, and therefore we regard them as illusory. This same conclusion is reached even when we view after-images with our eyes closed, since past experience has typically informed us that by closing the eyes external reality is "blotted-out," and that any images we continue to experience can only be attributed to internal events. Social factors can also enter into judgements about the origins of perceptual experiences, so that if the perceptions of one person do not correspond with those of a number of other persons, they may be regarded as "abnormal."

The noncorrespondence of certain aspects of experience with physically measured parameters of the external world leads us to the same conclusion that their origin is internal. The well-known Mach-band illusion is a case in point. Three boundaries of differential brightness are perceived instead of the single one expected to be generated by a single physically measur-

able step-function in light intensity. This phenomenon
and those of simultaneous color- and brightness-
contrast represent interactions between neural activity
across contours and can be explained as resulting from
lateral inhibition across networks of neurons (e.g., Békésy, 1967).

De Valois and Jacobs (1968) have shown that the perception of color depends upon differential rates of activity in visual cells that respond selectively to restricted
frequency-bands of light. In the lateral geniculate nucleus (a principal nucleus in the visual pathway from
the retina to the cortex) of the monkey there are four
types of color-sensitive neurons: "blue-on, yellow-
off"; "yellow-on, blue-off"; "red-on, green-off"; and
"green-on, red-off." All of these geniculate neurons fire
weakly in total darkness, and somewhat more strongly
in white light; but a "red-on, green off" cell, for
example, fires even more vigorously in red light and
ceases firing almost completely in green light. Comple-
mentary-colored after-images can be explained on the
basis of relative differences in activity of each group of
color-sensitive cells. Thus, if a red spot is steadily
fixated for thirty seconds and the gaze then diverted
elsewhere, a green after-image is perceived. During
fixation the array of cells in the lateral geniculate
nucleus with "red-on, green-off" characteristics will
have been fatigued in the region activated by the red
light. When a uniform field is then viewed, this fatigued region of cells will fire at a lower rate than "red-
on, green off" cells in other regions and will therefore
appear inhibited relative to the others, in the same way
as if a green light were actually present to inactivate it.
A converse, but similar, state of affairs exists simultaneously for the array of "green-on, red-off" cells.

Similar differentiating processes are involved in the perception of brightness. Differences in light intensity are directly related to nonchromatically sensitive arrays of differentially activated "light-on, dark-off" and "dark-on, light-off" neurons.

Therefore, we can understand how the concept of the light–dark dimension rests upon differentiating neural substrates. Osgood's (1952) semantic differentials probably correspond to various modes of differential neural activity. The oppositional nature of experience becomes comprehensible from this standpoint. If such dualistic oppositions as "light–dark," "cold–warm," "rough–smooth," or "loud–soft" depend upon differentiation within perceptual systems, it is not too difficult to conceive of the kinds of processes that must be involved in the genesis of higher-level, more abstract oppositions such as "good–bad," "heaven–hell," or "mind–body." Obviously, it would be foolhardy to speculate as to how such abstract oppositions involve more specific neural processes, given our fragmentary knowledge of the human brain. But in anthropology, total schemas of world knowledge incorporating the biological relativity of the human brain within them are currently being developed, as exemplified in the structuralism of Lévi-Strauss. The structuring of the world according to a matrix of binary oppositions is a universal characteristic of human thought and is regarded by Lévi-Strauss as a reflection of universal characteristics of human brain structure and function. The particular kinds of oppositions in thought that each culture selects are a function of the particular evolutionary history and biological adaptations of each culture.

The nervous system is only capable of differentiating *between* physical qualities; that is to say, one quality is compared relative to another, and no quality can be experienced *in itself*. It is for this reason the world is structured according to a matrix of binary oppositions. A single term can never have meaning in isolation, but acquires it by combination with its opposite. One term necessarily implies another, and the two in combination form a semantic unit.

If this function of the brain as a differentiating system is accepted, then it is clear that absolute knowledge of the external world is unattainable. Since sensory reception and discrimination are fundamentally related to biological survival, it follows that all knowledge must be biologically relative and not absolute.

Even the perception that the body itself is separate from the external world is relational. This relativity of feeling between the "out there" of the world and "in here" of our bodies undoubtedly depends upon the physiological distinction between exteroceptive and interoceptive neurons. Experience of the body as extended in space depends upon discontinuities in physical stimulation evoking differential activity in tactile and thermal exteroceptive neurons. Stimulation of the retina by light does not evoke any experience of the retina itself, but only of the external world, whereas touching the body with an object provokes a fused experience of the object itself and of the part of the body touched. Audition and olfaction, like sight, also do not evoke feelings of the body, but only of external events. The experience of the body as extended in space depends not only on the activity of tactile receptors distributed over the body surface, but also on patterns of proprioceptive activity that become correlated with patterns of efferent activity during development, as outlined in the previous chapter.

Boundaries of the body are experienced only when they are being discontinuously stimulated, either as a result of independent external pressures or of self-produced movement against a resistant object. As I sit here at this moment I can experience only those portions of my body that are subjected to discontinuous physical stimulation: my hands and arms resting on the surface of the table, my fingers holding the pen, my feet on the floor, and my buttocks on the chair. Other parts of my body are almost devoid of feeling unless I tense my muscles and thereby stimulate activity in proprioceptors. If a finger is dipped into water and held motionless, the pressure difference on the skin between the air and the water is felt at the line of demarcation between them—the surface of the water. Pressure around that part of the finger beneath the water is fairly uniform, as is the air pressure on the part of the finger above the water. Under certain conditions of "sensory deprivation," when the body is subjected to almost uniform stimulation throughout its surface, experience of it as an object localized in space can disappear. Various distortions and illusions of the body can arise, such as that of a "doppelgänger," in which the person feels that his mind has become detached from his body and has floated some distance away from it. The same kinds of "out of body" experiences can also occur during certain states of meditation in which the body is motionless and relaxed so as to reduce discontinuities in bodily stimulation.

The perception of space itself, surrounding and extending in depth beyond the body, depends upon only two sensory modalities—vision and audition, with vision being predominant in humans. In the absence of these two sensory modalities we would perceive "space" only to the extent that we perceive our bodies as spatial forms. Olfaction and taste do not generate experiences of space beyond the body, but only experiences localized at the body surfaces where the receptors are distributed.

It is significant to note that *pairs* of specialized sensory organs evolved for audition and vision (the eyes and ears, respectively). Again, differential activity, in this case between a pair of sense organs, is associated with the experience of three-dimensional space. Sounds are localized in space largely as a result of differences in the time of arrival, phase, and intensity of sound waves in the two ears.* Differences between these factors are systematically correlated with spatial location. Disparities between the images on each retina are resolved within the brain so as to yield the experience of stereopsis. Although experiences of depth can be achieved with monocular vision, the cues upon which such experience is based involve relative comparisons between activity in one part of the retina with another. The word "relative" inevitably crops up when one tries to describe monocular cues for space perception, which include relative size, texture, or perspective. Even the monocular cue of occlusion (which does not in itself yield a strong impression of depth) involves considerable learning and depends upon discontinuities in the relational patterns of afferent activity that underly contours.

---

*Although Batteau (1968) has demonstrated that sounds can be localized with one ear alone as a result of differences in phase between waves reflected from the asymmetrical pinna, it does not necessarily follow that this is the principal means by which sound is spatially localized under natural conditions. It could even be a learned ability dependent upon prior experience of the above factors using both ears.

Depth perception is described by Spengler as a creative *act* (1926, I:168f).

> From the moment of our awakening, the fateful and directed life appears in the phenomenal life as an experienced *depth*. Everything extends itself, but it is not yet "space," not something established in itself but a self-extension continued from the moving here to the moving there. World experience is bound up with the essence of *depth* (i.e., *farness* or *distance*). . . . This discrimination between the "third" and the other two dimensions, so called. . . , is inherent also in the opposition of the notions of sensation and contemplation. Extension into depth converts the former into the latter; in fact, depth is the first and genuine dimension in the literal sense of the word. In it the waking consciousness is active, whereas in the others it is strictly passive. The experience of depth . . . is an act, as entirely involuntary and necessary as it is creative, whereby the ego keeps the world, so to say, in subordination. Out of the rain of impressions the ego fashions a formal unit, a cinematic picture, which as soon as it is mastered by the understanding is subjected to law and the causality principle; and therefore, as the projection of an individual spirit it is transient and mortal.

This emphasis by Spengler on depth perception as an act is entirely consistent with psychophysiological knowledge on this subject. Perception of expansiveness (length and breadth) is given "passively" by the number of retinal units activated by a contour and does not require movement of the eyes or head. Although children born with sight in only one eye have depth perception based upon monocular cues, this ability requires motion of the body or head in order to produce the transformations in reafferent activity that yield the perception of depth, which undoubtedly requires considerable learning. Although under binocular conditions motions of the head or body are not necessary for

the creation of depth, an act is still required—that of
convergence of the eyes.

Neurons in the visual cortex of cats and monkeys are
not only selectively responsive to particular two-
dimensional features of planar forms, such as length and
orientation, but they also selectively respond to particular positions of those planar forms in depth (Barlow *et
al.*, 1967). When the eyes fixate on a stationary point in
space they converge at a certain angle. An object at a
distance greater or less than the fixation point will project an image onto each retina and the angular loci of the
two images (each measured relative to the fovea) will be
disparate. The angle of disparity bears an ordered relation to the distance of the object from the eyes. The
visual system is organized so that discrete sets of
neurons are activated by objects at various distances,
with each set corresponding to a particular retinal disparity. The cortical cells thus act as disparity detectors,
and the actual distances of the objects from the eyes are
calibrated relative to the angle of convergence of the
eyes. The system is much like a range finder in a cam-
era, which is constructed so that movement of the lens
backward and forward produces a systematically vary-
ing parallax between two split images of an object;
with zero parallax being produced by the object when
the image is brought into focus on the film.

In the visual system, as an object is moved closer and
closer, the eyes converge at progressively greater an-
gles in order to maintain zero disparity between the
foveal images, so that a particular set of cortical neurons
is excited by images with zero disparity. Hence the
perception of depth in animals capable of binocular vision depends upon the *act* of convergence and fixation
on an object in space.

Spengler argued that all aspects of a culture—as diverse as mathematics, science, art, and accounting practices—express the particular experience of depth of a people. It seems relevant here to note that the capacity for stereopsis reaches its highest level of development in the primates, and in humans in particular. It is generally accepted that the evolution of the ability to construct and use tools, which was crucial to the emergence of culture, depended on the evolution of an upright gait (which freed the hands) together with that of accurate binocular depth perception of objects held close to the body.

There is possibly one form of experience that does not rest on neural differentiation—the experience of time. The conclusion of Chapter 1 was that any analysis of time must be circular and that the analysis can begin with the concept of time as either a Kantian *a priori* intuition* or a physical entity. But regardless of one's starting point, the concept of time cannot be made dependent on relations. We cannot say that the experience of time arises from relations between physiological variables, because when we talk about relative concentrations of certain biochemicals, for example, we imply this to be at a given moment, presupposing the concept of a moment in time. The statement that relative concentrations of chemicals alter with time implies that time is something independent of those changes, although necessary for them to come about. The experience of time cannot be analyzed beyond saying that it arises internally, independent of any physically identifiable phenomena.

What neural processes are associated with the per-

---

*Kant argued that space, too, was an *a priori* intuition. But, as we have just seen, the perception of space depends on the existence of differential patterns of neural activity related to external physical events—conditions that are not necessary for the perception of time.

ception of motion? Frogs have feature detectors for movement in the optic tectum (Grusser-Cornehls *et al.*, 1963). These movement-detecting cells selectively respond to change in position of an image at two separate points on the retina within a limited time interval, so that a continuous sweep of the image across intervening areas of the retina is not required to perceive movement. The behavior of these neurons probably depends upon temporal summation of the activity of cells widely dispersed over the retina. Similar movement-sensitive neurons have also been found in the tectum and visual cortexes of mammals. The detection of motion therefore depends upon the activation of different neural arrays, but *in time* rather than simultaneously.

Thus, the perception of motion outside the organism is based upon the same sort of differential activity in the brain as is involved in other aspects of perception (except for time). It is not surprising, therefore, that Piaget (1966) reported that young children are capable of judging the speed of a moving object directly and do not appear to arrive at their judgements by conscious or unconscious computation of change of position with time as is done in computing velocity in mathematics. In other words, the perception of motion seems to be independent of the perception of time. The measurement of motion in physics by the use of time-measuring instruments involves different principles from those involved in the detection of motion by the nervous system. In fact, it is only through the prior existence of movement-sensitive feature detectors that the thought processes and operations of the physicist become possible.

Time and motion are thus distinct in neuropsychological analysis. It is only in physics that the two become interlinked, because of the particular method adopted for measuring, and therefore defining, time. Spengler put it another way when he wrote (1926, I:388):

> . . . the knowledge of Nature is an activity of *measurement*. All the same, we live even when we are observing and therefore the thing we are observing *lives with us*. The element in the Nature-picture in virtue of which it not merely from moment to moment *is*, but in a continuous flow with and around us *becomes*, is the copula of the waking consciousness and its world. This element is *called* movement, and it contradicts Nature as a picture. And therefore, as precisely as Understanding is abstracted (by means of words) from feeling and mathematical space from light-resistances ("things"), so also physical "time" is abstracted from the impression of motion.

Science attempts to explain nature in terms of a concatenation of simple motions. In so doing it can only describe a "dead Nature" or "nature become rigid," as Spengler put it, because it describes only motion "*in* the picture" and not motion "*of* the picture," which arises because of lived experience or biological time. For this reason, science cannot succeed in explaining evolution and history. Science constructs a rigid framework of laws, expressed in the form of mathematical equations in which time is excluded as a causal variable. Reversal of the sign t (time) in physical equations does not alter the pattern of events but only their directionality in time.

The philosophical implications of the differential neural processes underlying perception are profound. If knowledge of the world for each species, each human culture, and each human individual is related to its adaptive role in survival, then, as already indicated, the search for "truth" or absolute knowledge is in vain. As our environment and biological constitution change, so will our behavior, perceptions, and knowledge of the world change. It is an inevitable process in humans, being subjected as we are to the selective pressures of a rapidly changing environment—changes for which we ourselves are responsible.

We need only confine our attention to the history of science itself to see how one scientific theory is supplanted by another. Of course, this is due to a great extent to the evolution of theories and their application to the external world, as well as to the continuous expansion of our sensory capabilities in the form of scientific instruments. New scientific laws are created to account for new experiences. Thus Boyle's Law depended upon the prior development of the manometer for its formulation. Considered from the viewpoint of adaptation and survival, the evolution of scientific knowledge is like the evolution of sensory and perceptual abilities that occurs in all species. If we recognize the relativity of science to our own biological needs, we will avoid falling into the delusion that science constitutes knowledge of the world independent of our own bodily existence.

Einstein recognized the importance of the motion of an observer relative to the purported object of his experience in formulations of laws of physics. But we need to go a step further—into the brain itself—and incorporate models of brain function into our models of the physical world, since models of the physical world depend upon the prior existence of the brain. The brain must be considered as a modifier or limiter of the descriptions it yields by its own operations. Original perceptions of the world are translated into formulations about the properties of the physical world in the form of laws that influence subsequent perceptions of the world, and these in turn, through the intellectual operations of the brain, lead to further formulations and so on in an endless circular progression of ideas. From the perspective of psychobiology, this circular progression is considered adaptive, as one aspect of an overall evolutionary process. But, to be self-consistent, the psychobiological analysis must itself be regarded as another aspect of the same evolutionary process, and therefore as biologically relative and circular as the physical analysis.

5   Consciousness

It is often thought that physiological events have an existence separate from that of conscious experience. But it should be recognized that "physiological events" are scientific formulations that represent the experiences of physiologists. That is to say, physiological events are experiences obtained in the physiological laboratory, often through the use of specialized electronic equipment. In short, physiological events are a *special category of experience.* In this chapter I shall examine some relations between physiological events and other categories of experience—behavior in particular.

Behavior and physiology are not completely separate concepts. Both involve movement of matter in space.

But behavior involves the movement of larger aggregates of matter than does physiology. In addition, behavior is universally accessible to observation,* whereas the observation of physiological phenomena—which was made possible only relatively recently—is largely restricted to those individuals who have access to the necessary sensing instruments. Because of their special "vision," these individuals have developed a specialized language of experience that has no meaning for those untrained in the discipline. If we possessed "X-ray eyes" so that we could directly observe the physiological events occurring in one another's bodies, descriptions of ourselves and others would be heavily laden with physiological terms. If we could directly observe electroencephalographic (EEG) alpha rhythms in the brain, then (for reasons I shall discuss shortly) we would naturally assume that a person was relaxed whenever we saw alpha rhythms appear. Under such fictional circumstances we might use the term "alpha" instead of "relax" and describe a person as "alphaed." Certainly, the relatively recent development of psychoanalysis has influenced everyday descriptions of behavior and experience, which often include such terms as "ego," "id," and "libido," terms that were originally introduced by Freud to refer to processes that he assumed had a physiological reality.

So far the closest correlations between neurophysiological events and other aspects of experience have been established in sensory processes, through studies by Mountcastle (1967) and Stevens (1957) among others. For example, Mountcastle has shown

---

*"Behavior" is distinguished from physiology in this book by being considered as patterns of *external* bodily movement.

that physical pressure applied to the surface of the skin is related by a power function to both neural activity in the somatosensory systems of monkeys and experienced pressure in humans. Mountcastle's results also showed that the brain as a whole acts as a linear operator and has no effect on the shape of the power function, which is set by the process of sensory transduction at the primary sensory receptor. The power function is the same at the level of the primary tactile receptor as at the somatosensory cortex. On the other hand, the shape of the power function differs for different sensory receptors, so that the eye does "see" and the skin "feel," since, at least in terms of such primary qualities as intensity of physical stimulation, the brain does not modify the mathematical transformation function between physical stimulation and neural activity established at the receptor.

Systematic psychophysiological relations between anatomical pathways and perceptual experiences also exist. The association of various areas in the brain with specific modalities of sensory experience is well known, so that such terms as "visual," "auditory," or "somatosensory" cortex have become standard in usage. Topographic relations between anatomical pathways and perceptual fields have also been established. Brain lesions, depending on their location, result in specific losses in perceptual abilities. The well-known experiments by Penfield and Rasmussen (1950) involving brain stimulation of conscious human patients undergoing brain surgery produced considerable evidence for topographic relations between the brain and perceptual experiences.

These anatomical and physiological relations between afferent processes and perceptual experience are consistent with the traditional assumption that perception is a passive process, largely dependent on patterns of afferent activity. However, the finding that vision disappears if the image on the retina is artificially stabilized (Ditchburn and Ginsborg, 1952; Riggs *et al.*, 1953), together with studies of perceptual development and perceptual disarrangement (Held, 1965), have compelled recognition of the importance of motor activity as a critical component of the perceptual process. Indeed, Festinger and Cannon (1965) proposed an efferent theory of perception opposite to the traditional one in which programs of afferent activity are considered to be dominant. According to this theory, even in situations in which there is no overt movement by the organism, the readiness or preparedness to move underlies perception. A conflict therefore exists between theories of perception based primarily on afferent activity and those based primarily on efferent activity. I shall now argue that both extreme views are false; that they arose through a confusion in the interpretation of "subjective" and "objective" experience, which can be resolved when these categories of experience are logically related to each other.

Kant argued that the *perceived* world constitutes the *knowable* world. The world as a "thing in itself" is beyond the reach of our senses—a noumenon. Therefore, to talk about "objective" experience as referring to any kind of absolute external reality is illogical. When we talk about "objective" experience we are referring to the world as perceived by a group of persons who share similar physical locations and physiological systems. When we talk about "subjective" experience we are referring to the world experienced (and described) by other persons considered as objects of study. Another way of describing the situation is to refer to "frames of reference," like those represented in Figure 16.

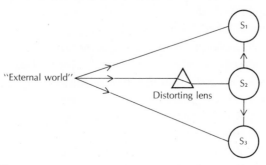

FIGURE 16

The three circles S_1, S_2, and S_3, represent the perceptions of three people. If all three brains "infer" the same "external world," their experiences will be similar and considered to represent "objective reality." If, however, S_1 and S_2 both observe S_3 as part of their external world, a divergence between the experience of S_3 and that common to S_1 and S_2 (which now includes the behavior of S_3) may result, either because of experimental manipulations (such as putting distorting spectacles on S_3) or because the brain activity of S_3 no longer corresponds to that of S_1 and S_2 owing to a change in attitude in the latter two. S_1 and S_2 now call the experience of S_3 "subjective" and their own "objective." This relativism of experience has been recognized by psychoanalysts such as Szasz (1961) and Laing (1967) but has not extended very far beyond the field of psychiatry to the study of perception in general. Once it is understood that the distinction between "subjective" and "objective" depends upon the relative viewpoints of observers, then it is possible to proceed to an understanding of the relation between afferent and efferent processes in perception.

Festinger and his colleagues (1970) found that when the visual system is disarranged relative to the rest of the body by looking through prismatic spectacles (so that, for example, straight rods appear curved to the subject), greater perceptual adaptation occurs when new afferent–efferent associations are learned than when they are not. Let us examine the results of these experiments, taking the relative observational standpoints of the experimenter and subject into account. When the prisms are placed in front of the subject's eyes by the experimenter, two parallel rods straight in every respect for the experimenter cast (in the experimenter's experience) an image on the subject's retina like that which normally results from a curved rod. But the subject cannot observe the image of the rods on his own retina. To him the rods initially look curved and even feel curved when he runs his fingers along them. After some exposure to this situation, perceptual adaptation takes place and the rods progressively appear less and less curved, both tactually and visually.

The traditional interpretation of such effects of perceptual disarrangement has been to regard the afferent visual information as dominant in the determination of perceptual experience (e.g., Gibson, 1933). Instead, Festinger and his colleagues interpreted the subject's initial experience of curviness to be due to a change in programs of efferent activities transmitted to the arm because of the altered visual afferent pattern; the new efferent activities override the proprioceptive information received reafferently by the arm and hand in running a stylus between the "objectively" straight rods. Festinger and his colleagues connect consciousness with the efferent rather than the afferent system— the afferent visual activity influences consciousness only through its effects on programs of efferent activity. In opposition to these conclusions, I shall argue that by altering visual information one alters motor activity (including speech), so that associating consciousness with any one particular segment of the total neural process is not justified.

Emphasis must be placed on the reorganization of efferent activity *relative* to afferent visual activity. Different patterns of speech, considered as efferent activity, are brought about by different patterns of afferent activity. In other words, if visual information is altered, the intellectual content of statements that refer to visual information will be altered accordingly. In any disarrangement of previously established relations between sensory and motor activity, vision is dominant if the visual information forms the reference point around which the motor activity is newly organized. The test of perceptual adaptation for the subject in Festinger's experiment was to set the rods, by turning a knob that caused them to bend to various degrees, so that they appeared *visually* straight to him. Adaptation was said to have occurred if the subject set the rods so that they appeared less curved to the experimenter than when initially set by the subject immediately after he first put on the prismatic lenses.

Let us analyze further what is going on during adaptation. The subject is aware that he has been given distorting lenses, so naturally he realizes that his visual information has been interfered with. Wearing the distorting spectacles he realizes that he now does not share the same visual conditions with other persons and that he must try to relate his language to nonvisual information if he is to communicate effectively. Therefore, when given the opportunity to feel objects, he will trust his tactile and proprioceptive reafferent activity as representing "external reality" more closely than his visual information. Accordingly, he will recalibrate his visual activity relative to the reafferent activity originating in his hand and arm, taking the latter as the common reference for communication by language.

Such experiments on perceptual disarrangement in which language is involved in effect represent *sociocultural experiments*. The subject recalibrates his visual images along the semantic dimension of "straight–curved," with his language anchored in the reafferent activity generated by his hand and arm movements. Later, the subject is tested in a situation in which only visual information is provided, and the experimenter assesses the degree to which this recalibration has taken place. In accordance with this interpretation, in Festinger's experiments greater recalibration occurred when subjects were allowed to "feel" the rods (by moving a stylus up and down between them) than when they were not. But the fact that active movement was involved in the learning of new afferent–efferent associations does not logically lead one to the conclusions of Festinger and his colleagues that consciousness depends principally upon the efferent portion of the total process.

The importance of reafferent activity generated by arm and hand movements involved in feeling an object is readily recognized. But it is not always realized (because we are not consciously aware of it) that the eye, too, can "feel." Gibson (1966) has pointed this out by noting the proprioceptive aspects of the retina. When we look at a black dot on a white surface and then move our eyes in different directions, each pattern of efferent activity (eye movement) produces movement of the dot's image on the retina and a correlated pattern of afferent visual activity. In this respect the propriocep-tive function of the eyes is not different from that of the limbs. Under certain circumstances the eyes can, so to speak, "feel" a visual distortion just as well, if not bet-ter, than the hand.

For example, in one of the experiments performed by Festinger and his colleagues a prism was mounted di-rectly on a contact lens worn by subjects, who were allowed the use of only one eye. The subjects were presented with two parallel rods that could be bent by the experimenter so that they initially appeared to be either straight or curved to the subject. In this situation, in order to maintain a sharp image of the rods on the fovea, the subject's eye had to move along a path con-forming to the experimenter's retinal image rather than one corresponding to the subject's. Although the sub-jects' experiences were not described, one can imagine what they were. When the subject is presented with a rod that appears curved to him but straight to the exper-imenter, he must, if he is to maintain fixation along the entire rod, move his eyes along a "straight" path. If he moves his eyes along the curved path that conforms to his own retinal image, loss of fixation will result be-cause the prism will shift the position of the image of the rod on the retina either up or down (depending on the direction of the curvature on the image). When pre-sented with a rod that appears curved to the experi-menter but straight to the subject, the opposite condi-tions obtain.

Under normal everyday conditions the eye usually moves in a series of approximately straight saccadic motions and rarely in a continuous motion. Therefore, it can readily be understood why the observed adaptation to the prism was greatest for the condition in which the subject viewed a rod apparently curved to him but straight to the experimenter. When viewing such a rod it is easier for the subject to continue his accustomed straight saccadic movements of the eyes, thereby keeping the rod in focus, than to try to track the "spurious" curved retinal information. By retaining his customary straight saccadic eye movements, corresponding to those in persons not subject to such visual disarrangement, he can consider them still related to the word "straight." Under the condition in which he views a rod that appears straight to himself but curved to the experimenter, the subject is forced to execute curved eye movements in order to maintain fixation on the rod. As a result, the subject is forced to relinquish the straight saccadic efferent patterns that he shares with other, normal persons (including of course the experimenter) and so does not have any information in common with the experimenter to which he can refer the word "straight." In this condition he is much more at sea and exhibits less adaptation. Consistent with this interpretation is the additional finding that adaptation to both conditions was less when the experimenter moved a pointer along the rods in a continuous motion so as to induce curved smooth-pursuit eye movements.

During evolution and individual development, patterns of afferent activity originating in different sensory systems become correlated. These correlations may be established in the absence of any specific efferent activity, as I described earlier in the discussion of sensory–sensory learning. But sensory activity of different modalities can also become unified in experience as a result of motor activity. Thus, running a finger along a rod requires a specific efferent program maintaining tactile and/or visual contact of the finger with the rod. Movement of the finger evokes activity in tactile receptors and proprioceptors, such as joint receptors and muscle spindles. Theoretically, the activity involved in the continuous tracking of a rod with the finger could be described mathematically by a matrix of functional equations relating the activities in each of the different efferent and afferent systems. This matrix would also bear a formal relation to the system of efferent programs underlying the language of each culture. If a structural alteration occurs in any one of these systems of activity, then the previously established transformation functions between the other systems and the altered system of activity are no longer valid and the altered system must be recalibrated, relative to the others.

Although programs of efferent activity are critically involved in perception, as pointed out by Festinger and his colleagues, their involvement is *relative* to patterns of afferent activity. The extent of their involvement changes with the phenomenal perspective taken— whether that of the subject or experimenter. Efferent processes seem to predominate over afferent processes from the perspective of the experimenter since it is only by way of the former that he can gain any information concerning the subject's experiences. From the perspective of the subject, however, perception can be based exclusively upon afferent activity, (although the efferent pathway generates reafferent activity which would otherwise not be obtained). Correlations between afferent and reafferent activity patterns then determine subsequent patterns of efferent activity, including speech.

If other experiments on perceptual disarrangement—such as the classic one by Stratton (1897) in which the entire visual field was optically inverted—were interpreted using the conceptual frame of reference schematized in Figure 16, many of the past difficulties in interpreting their results should disappear. Instead of basing perceptual experience predominantly upon patterns of either afference or efference, the relations between activity in each physiological system should be determined, and these in turn related to expressions of speech. Such an analysis would extend the relativistic approach developed by Einstein for physical events to physiological and psychological events.

So far I have considered the relations between neural activity in local regions of the brain and aspects of individual experience during what is considered to be a single, uniform state of consciousness—wakefulness. But if experience is closely related to patterns of brain activity, then we would expect it to alter markedly whenever patterns of neural activity throughout the entire brain change, as when a person falls asleep.

Although early investigations of experience during sleep and wakefulness yielded results that supported this expectation, subsequent work did not, so that close correspondence between alterations in overall brain activity and alterations in experience have yet to be established. I believe the reason for the difficulty in finding such correspondence rests on limitations in our ability to have direct access to experience during states of consciousness other than the one in which we are performing the analysis. In the ensuing discussion I shall show that these limitations arise because of uncertainty as to whether or not we have accurate memories of experiences that occurred during states of consciousness other than the one we are currently experiencing, and because of our inability to communicate by means of language from some states of consciousness to others. These limitations in memory and communication lead to the concept of "state-specific" knowledge, which has developed from certain considerations of sleep and drug-induced states of consciousness.

Although the physiological and behavioral distinctions between sleep and wakefulness are reasonably clear cut (Berger, 1969a), the differences in ongoing experience are not so distinct. It is often claimed that consciousness is lost during sleep, but the results of recent laboratory investigations indicate that mental activity of some kind can usually be reported following awakenings from any stage in the sleep cycle, although the quality of this mental activity varies greatly with the stage. The reported experiences can range all the way from the recollection that one was dreaming but without being able to recall any specific content, through vague thoughts or isolated visual images, to the richness of detail of a vivid dream with all its characteristic imagery and emotional feelings (Berger, 1969b).

Unfortunately, it is extremely difficult to identify any unique characteristics of dreams that differentiate them from waking experiences. Hall and Nordby (1972) were unable to do so from studies of thousands of dreams and thus have emphasized the essential continuity between waking and dream thought. The fact that the dreamer himself is usually able to distinguish his dreams from waking experiences might be considered sufficient evidence that certain distinctions must exist between the two experiences. But the question remains whether the ability to distinguish between dreaming and waking experiences is based on actual differences between the qualities of the dream and waking experiences or the behavioral and environmental context of waking up. The fact that the dreamer awakens to find himself in bed in a darkened bedroom may be sufficient for him to conclude that any prior experiences that could not logically have taken place in that room must have occurred in a dream. Sometimes it does happen that a person awakens from sleep and for some moments cannot tell whether he is experiencing a dream or wakefulness until he "gathers himself together" by taking account of his surroundings. Recalled feelings and attitudes in nightmares certainly indicate that the dreamer treats them as "real," at the time they occurred, as he treats waking experiences.*

However, dreams do differ from waking life in one crucial aspect. In wakefulness we are able to reflect on events not directly connected with contemporaneous events and actions. In a dream, however, we do not spontaneously recall earlier events in the dream unless the events are directly connected with an ongoing purpose or action. For example, while driving home from a party in a dream, we would not passively meditate on events at the party—we would not "run them through our mind." There are occasions in dreams in which the dreamer returns somewhere to retrieve an object left behind, so that memory of prior events in the dream can occur. But *reminiscence* in dreams does not occur.

Furthermore, dreams in which a person recalls earlier waking experiences and recognizes them as such do not

---

*Occasionally, the dreamer may "realize" during dreaming that he is dreaming. But there have not been any experiments to determine whether or not these instances are accompanied by momentary physiological awakenings during which perception of one or more aspects of the physical surroundings furnish a context that allows the person to conclude that he or she is dreaming.

occur. By contrast, during wakefulness we recall dreams and regard them as memories of experiences that occurred earlier while we were asleep.

The fact that dreams are usually quickly forgotten, even when recalled soon after awakening, represents another difference between sleep and waking memory. Try to recall a dream you experienced over a year ago. I cannot. Yet I can recall in considerable detail countless seemingly insignificant events that happened in the same time when I was awake. Why should this typical difference between memory of dream and waking events exist? It is not as though the dream events are phenomenonally any less "real" or vivid than waking events at the time they are experienced. They often have even more impact than waking experiences. Nevertheless, they fade away in a similar manner to fictional events in novels. Of course, great writers have the ability to depict certain scenes that make a lasting impression on memory, but striking events in dreams can also make indelible impressions throughout life. Although dreams typically have a vivid visual quality, films or plays generally instil stronger memories than dreams or novels. Perhaps the fact that plays and films are experienced through *iconic* stimulation of the sensory systems, whereas dreams and novels are not, may help to explain some of the differences in ability to remember each.

Let us turn now to empirical data relating to memory processes during sleep. All studies on learning during sleep in which physiological variables were recorded show that people are unable to clearly remember auditory events occurring during sleep itself. Any memories that do arise are of events that occurred at times when the person was physiologically awake for at least a few seconds. For example, in one study on verbal learning during sleep, the only words learned were those that happened to have been presented during brief episodes of physiological wakefulness (Koukkou and Lehmann, 1968). Although external events that occur during sleep are not normally remembered during wakefulness,* some discriminative recognition does take place during sleep. For example, Oswald and his colleagues (1960) found that sleeping subjects awakened more easily to their own spoken name or those of friends than to names having no special meaning to them spoken at the same intensity. The awakening of a mother to the cry of her baby, but not to the noise of a train, is an everyday example of this discriminative ability. Therefore, the absence of learning during sleep does not depend upon any deficiency in the ability to discriminate one sensation from another. The deficiency must reside in the faculty of memory itself. Although when awake we do not ordinarily remember external events that occurred during sleep, we often do remember those internal events that we call dreams. What factors determine whether or not we remember dreams?

During sleep, because of the inhibition of motor activity, reinforcement of *behavior* cannot occur as in wakefulness. The only reinforcement that can take place during sleep is that of afferent–afferent associations. During sleep the brain is largely decoupled from the environment. The conditions of lying relatively motionless in a soft bed at a uniform temperature in a quiet, darkened bedroom approach those of sensory-deprivation experiments. There is very little externally

---

*A special kind of waking memory of external events occurring during physiologically defined sleep takes place when the external events become incorporated into dream imagery. But distortion of these incorporated external events almost invariably occurs, so that the dream memory does not constitute memory of the actual events themselves (Berger, 1963).

evoked afferent or internally evoked reafferent activity. If afferent–afferent reinforcement occurs during dreams, there is no reason to suppose that it should differ from that which occurs during wakefulness.

Although afferent–afferent associations formed during dreams do allow a person to recall dream events during wakefulness, they do not facilitate recall *during* the dream of earlier events *within* the dream itself. The reason for this difference may lie to some extent in the decoupling of the brain from the environment during sleep. The brain cannot respond with motor activity to afferent activity during dreaming because of powerful motor inhibition. Therefore, there is no way in which efferent activity can evoke reafferent activity and thereby establish an objective present by actual interaction with the environment. During wakefulness, on the other hand, we are able to differentiate perceptions from dreams, reflections, and fantasies by interacting with the physical environment. On awakening from a dream we may attempt to feel a familiar bed or a bedside table, and if we receive the anticipated patterns of reafferent activity, this confirmation of our expectancies locks us into a known environment and provides us with an existential domain to which our dreams, memories, and fantasies can be compared. Our inability to perform these actions during sleep explains our associated inability to discriminate whether an experience is "really happening" (i.e., is anchored within a "reafferent present") or whether it is a memory or fantasy. In dreams we cannot be aware that we are recollecting earlier associations because an existential present cannot be created through actual interaction with the environment. Within dreams history does not exist, and in that respect dreams are timeless.

A final point relevant to this discussion is the usual absence of the recognition by the dreamer himself that he is "having a dream." The memory of having gone to bed is not experienced during dreaming, as it is on awakening. Although dream experiences have their origins in events occurring earlier in the life of the dreamer, as Freud (1953) was the first to elaborate, this historical foundation of dreams is not *consciously recognized* during the dreams themselves and is recognized only to a limited extent during subsequent wakefulness. At the time it occurs, the dream world is complete in itself, and the origin of its events in another state of existence is not recognized, no doubt because of the aforementioned differences between memory processes during sleeping and waking.

Early studies on the dichotomy between rapid-eye-movement (REM) and nonrapid-eye-movement (NREM) sleep and dream recall strongly indicated that memory of dreams was an exclusive property of REM sleep (e.g., Dement and Kleitman, 1957).* In fact, the

---

*Associated with the well-known behavioral characteristics of sleep are marked alterations in most physiological variables (Berger, 1969a). Alterations in the patterns of electroencephalographic (EEG) activity of the brain are among the most striking of these physiological changes. When a person relaxes, his EEG typically changes from a high-frequency, low-voltage pattern associated with active attentive behavior to one of almost continuous 8–10 cycles per second sinusoidal alpha rhythm. The alpha rhythm becomes even slower in frequency and slightly higher in voltage when a person becomes drowsy. As sleep is entered, there is a progressive increase in high-voltage 0.5–2 cycles per second slow-wave activity. During certain recurrent periods in sleep the EEG reverts back to a pattern similar to that seen during the initial onset of sleep, but these periods are accompanied by distinctive binocularly conjugate rapid eye movements, which are quite different from the slow, rolling side-to-side movements that typically occur during sleep onset. It is for this reason that these recurrent episodes of sleep have been called rapid-eye-movement (REM) sleep.

excitement provoked by the initial discovery of REM sleep by Aserinsky and Kleitman (1953) lay in the belief that a close correlation had at last been found between physiological variables and specific experiences. But subsequent studies, especially those of Foulkes (1966), indicated that the identification of dreaming with REM sleep was inaccurate. Definitive dreams indistinguishable from typical REM dreams can sometimes be recalled on awakening from the initial NREM period of the night before any REM sleep has occurred, as well as after awakenings from NREM periods immediately subsequent to awakenings from REM periods in which dreams were reported. These NREM dream reports cannot be explained away as representing reminiscences of earlier REM dreams and one has to conclude that at least a definite, though small, number of dreams occur during NREM sleep.

However, the question remains as to whether those differences in quality and frequency of dream reports that have been observed following REM and NREM awakenings are a reflection of the incidence and type of mental activity actually occurring during REM and NREM sleep, or whether they might reflect differences in the ability to recall dreams that have essentially the same quality and frequency in both sleep phases. Putting it another way, does dreaming itself wax and wane during sleep in association with the REM–NREM sleep cycle or does memory of uniformly occurring dreams alter with sleep state, creating a semblance of changes in the nature of dreaming itself? This is a difficult problem to resolve and one that I have dealt with at some length elsewhere (Berger, 1967, 1969b). What I wish to emphasize here is the light thrown upon memory processes during sleep by a number of experiments focused on differences in dream recall following awakenings from REM and NREM sleep.

A clear-cut and relevant finding is the rapid decline in frequency of dream recall following the end of a REM period as awakenings are made progressively later during the ensuing NREM period. There are two possible explanations for this result. One is that the REM dream events are not consolidated in memory during subsequent NREM sleep and can only exist in short-term memory, so that they are usually irretrievably lost within ten minutes from the end of the REM period. Another possibility is that both REM and NREM dreams are consolidated in long-term memory during sleep but that only REM dreams are accessible to recall on awakening, because of "state-dependency" of memory resulting from the greater difference between the physiology of NREM sleep and wakefulness than between that of REM sleep and wakefulness.

Consistent with the memory consolidation hypothesis are the results of studies by Portnoff and colleagues (1966) and Goodenough and colleagues (1971) in which subjects were awakened several times during the night and shown words. They were then either permitted to return to sleep immediately or were kept awake for a few minutes. Memory of the words was tested the following morning and was poorer when the subjects had returned immediately to NREM sleep than when they had been kept awake. This finding points toward an inability to consolidate memories of waking events during subsequent NREM sleep. The same inability may pertain to consolidation of REM dreams during subsequent NREM sleep. On the other hand, if differences in memory consolidation underlie the differences in dream recall, then one should not be able to obtain

reports of extended dreams following NREM awakenings. Yet these do occur with a definite though small
frequency. In order to account for this fact one has to
postulate the existence of considerable variability in
memory consolidation during NREM sleep, which presents no clear advantage over the postulation of variation in the occurrence of dreams between REM and
NREM sleep.

Instead, let us consider the state-dependency hypothesis. This hypothesis as applied to dream recall
represents an extension of the state-dependency of
memory on the physiological conditions produced by
different drugs (Overton, 1964). Briefly, if an animal
learns a task under the influence of a particular drug,
recall of the task is better when the animal is subsequently tested in the same drugged condition than
when it is tested in the normal, nondrugged state. The
same effect applies to humans (Goodwin *et al.*, 1969;
Hill *et al.*, 1973). The effect is also drug-specific, so that
it is not a question of all drug states being equivalent as
compared with the nondrugged state.

The physiological state of the brain and body during
REM sleep is similar to that of wakefulness, both of
which differ considerably from that of NREM sleep.
Therefore, in accordance with the state-dependency
hypothesis of learning, one would expect recall during
wakefulness to be better for prior events that occurred
during REM sleep than for prior events that occurred
during NREM sleep.

The observed differences in frequency of recall of
dreams following awakenings from REM and NREM
sleep are therefore consistent with the state-dependency hypothesis, as is the progressive decrease in frequency of recall following the end of a REM period,
since the transition from REM to NREM sleep is a

gradual one and not a step-function. Differences in the ability to recall dream events from the two sleep stages might also account for the differences in the quality of dreams. NREM dreams tend to be shorter, more fragmentary and lack the vivid quality that REM dreams typically possess—analogous to the faded memory of a novel read several years previously, when little more than a general idea or theme can be recalled.

What can be concluded about the nature of memory during sleep? It seems fairly safe to say that veridical memory of external events does not occur. Memory during wakefulness of dream events is good for REM sleep but probably impaired for NREM sleep, even though it is likely that dreams do occur during NREM sleep. Reminiscence *within* dreams about earlier dream or waking events does not seem to occur, although further research is necessary to substantiate this claim. The dream represents a continuous unfolding of events and does not appear to involve reflective processes as in wakefulness. Sleep, therefore, does not appear to be a particularly useful state for establishing physiological correlates of specific experiences, since the stream of experiences seems to flow unceasingly through the 24-hour period.

The principle difference between dreaming and waking experience is *contextual*, and involves *analysis* dependent on memory—the reflective process whereby one event is related and compared to another. Little analysis occurs in dreams, where events simply unfold. Their relative significance is not analyzed as in waking thought. Proust showed how experience through the process of memory influences present waking experience. But in dreams the "past" does not even seem to exist.

An examination of causality in dreams as compared to

wakefulness might also prove helpful in the search for an understanding of consciousness. In a sense Freud has already performed such an examination. His conclusions were formulated essentially in terms of the Pleasure and Reality Principles (Freud, 1964). The dream, as viewed by Freud (1953) is the occasion for the fullest expression of the libido in accord with the Pleasure Principle, whereas wakefulness requires the curbing of libidinal impulses according to the Reality Principle.

When Freud initially developed the idea of the Unconscious, it must have appeared to many as a contradiction in terms. How could something that was not conscious affect consciousness, and yet be *mental* rather than physical (i.e., physiological)? Something that was not conscious and yet was also not physical appeared to violate Cartesian dualism. Because nothing could exist outside either the mental or the physical category and because consciousness was mental, there was no domain within which the Unconscious could exist. Therefore, the Unconscious was a contradiction in terms.

Freud attempted to resolve this self-contradiction by extending the concept of the "mental" to include events other than those that directly entered consciousness and considered the dream to be the "royal road to the Unconscious." Translating Freud's psychological terms into biological terms, the Id can be represented as the genotype, which expresses itself most freely during dreams following the Pleasure Principle, whereas the Ego can be represented as the phenotype, which functions during wakefulness and obeys the Reality Principle. Since the sleeping personality or genotype provides the foundation upon which the waking personality or phenotype comes into existence, the sleeping personality serves the waking personality. But the two are actually interdependent in that the waking personality serves the sleeping personality by preserving the body, in which the genotype resides. However, I shall now argue that, from the standpoint of behavioral adaptation, the waking personality needs to take account of the sleeping personality (if only indirectly), but not vice versa, and that this asymmetry in function may account for the existence of unidirectional memory from sleep to wakefulness. In other words, the asymmetry in memory between dreaming and waking experience may be a manifestation of the biological principle of self-preservation.

The waking personality must be concerned with "realities," since the nature of wakeful functions, to use Piaget's (1952) terms, is to assimilate certain aspects of the environment and accommodate to others in the interest of bodily preservation. The Reality Principle refers to those cognitions that are crucial to the preservation of bodily existence and involved in predictive learning. Predictive learning establishes certain relations between perceived events, and often has the utility of successfully predicting future perceptions brought about by the animal's own actions. This internal ordering of perceived events is projected by humans onto the external world in various forms, one of which is the concept of *causality*. Causality thus provides yeoman's service toward bodily survival. But in dreams our brains are detached from the physical environment so that the opportunity for efferent–reafferent reinforcement is absent. Therefore, perceptual analysis, in the form of, say, causality cannot be put to a practical test during sleep. What takes place during dreams is an

expression of the degree to which the genotypic sleeping personality has actualized itself in the waking personality. Moreover, following the Pleasure Principle,
new ways of realizing as yet unfulfilled potentials in the
genotype (many of which are universally common to
humans and represent Jung's Collective Unconscious)
can be explored during dreams by recording patterns of
afferent activity. These mental explorations constitute
the *creative* aspect of dreams that Jung (1906b) emphasized. The potentialities of actualizing the genotype
explored in dreams can subsequently be attempted by
the waking personality according to the Reality Principle. The reverse process is not possible, which accounts
for the unidirectional quality of memory from sleep to
wakefulness.

The solution to the apparent paradox of Freud's Unconscious is that it is not in fact "unconscious." Instead,
it constitutes a different form of consciousness, one that
runs rampant during sleep and which we are only dimly
aware of when we are awake (and unfortunately tend to
dismiss too readily as "irrelevant"). In fact, the concept
of the Unconscious is arrived at through consciousness,
a reversal of classical ideas concerning the phylo-
genesis and ontogenesis of consciousness. It is only
through consciousness that the Unconscious comes into
existence.

Communication 6

When we are awake, as you and I are now, our consciousness depends upon the physiological conditions of wakefulness. At the same time, we are restricted in our ability to communicate by the limitation of the language process to these physiological conditions. During sleep and certain other states of consciousness this ability to communicate is lost. Tart (1972) has argued that for each particular physiological state there exists an associated psychological state, and that knowledge as epitomized in science has become identified with only one of the possible states—normal non-drugged wakefulness. Other physiological states yield their own special kinds of experience and knowledge, each of which is valid for that particular state.

What we ordinarily mean by "knowledge" is that which can be put into language. Knowledge thus becomes an exclusive property of wakefulness, since communication by language is limited to wakefulness. If we talk about experiences that purportedly occurred during other states of consciousness, such as sleep, we are in effect analyzing our *memories* of those other states. And since our memories are embedded in the physiological conditions of wakefulness, they are probably distorted by the conditions peculiar to wakefulness. They cannot therefore be a true re-presentation of the experiences as they actually occurred during the other states. Tart has suggested that state-specific knowledge obtained by traditional methods of science should be possible for states of consciousness other than normal wakefulness, in particular for drug-induced states of consciousness.* Speech continues in many drug-induced states, so that it should be possible to generate, by analysis, experimentation, and communication within those states, a self-contained body of knowledge specific to those states. That is to say, all the investigators and readers of their work would have to take the same drug. But because communication by language is not possible during sleep and certain other states, a definitive body of knowledge specific to these states cannot exist. It is small wonder, then, that

---

*Differences in state-specific consciousness should not be confused with differences in waking consciousness between different cultures, as described by anthropologists, and which I shall discuss shortly. The physiology of the human brain is basically the same in all mankind. Differences in cultural outlook are at least partially communicable from one culture to another if a person from one culture lives in another culture for a considerable period. In Samuel Butler's country of "Erewhon" the concepts of religion, justice, punishment, and health are inverted from their usual meanings in Western civilization. Butler illustrated how irrational thoughts are universal to human beings but construed within each culture to be rational. The same essential conclusions have been drawn by Benedict (1959) and by Lévi-Strauss from their anthropological observations.

paranormal experiences are often incomprehensible in waking consciousness, especially for people who have never experienced them. Even dreams do not "exist" for persons who never remember them and who cannot imagine what it is like to "dream." Even those of us who do remember them perceive them through the dark glass of Freud's Secondary Elaboration process.

Having dealt with the physiological limitations that different states of consciousness impose upon our ability to communicate with one another I shall now focus on less trivial aspects of language and their implications for an understanding of consciousness. Namely, the influence the form and meaning of language has upon the form and mode of consciousness.

Since this is a written work employing language, it is impossible for me to step outside the domain of language and yet continue to communicate with you the reader. That is, it is impossible to talk about language without using language itself, and again we find ourselves trapped within a circle. In an analysis of language, language must chase its own tail. All that can be done at this point is see to what degree language is internally consistent. That is to say, we need to examine whether a conceptual system by which certain rules are generated obeys those same rules itself.

Maturana (1970) has emphasized the importance of the imperative, or orienting, function of language. Language orients a listener toward a certain pattern of afferent activity that a speaker has chosen to isolate from his total background of afferent activity. Language tends to create mutual patterns of afferent activity in speaker and listener. These patterns can originate externally from environmental events or internally from events within the body and brain. But, as Maturana has pointed out, the meaning communicated by language resides in the listener rather than in the speaker. The patterns of brain activity that are created in the listener represent the meaning of the communication *to him* and do not necessarily correspond with the patterns of afferent activity that the speaker has chosen to represent in words. In other words, language is not a form of communication whereby information is transmitted from one person to another in any absolute manner. What is communicated depends upon relative patterns of activity in the brains of the speaker and the listener; it is therefore a function of the genotypic and phenotypic history of each.

The development of language is grounded in perception. The first words infants understand and speak are nouns. Since innate visual feature detectors can be selectively responsive to movements of stimuli in specific directions as well as to their specific shapes, whereas other feature detectors have not been discovered that selectively respond to the conjunction of separate contours, it is not surprising that intransitive verbs such as "walk" or "sit" are learned prior to transitive verbs such as "hit" (Macnamara, 1972). Other attributes of objects, such as their color, evoke activity in other specific populations of neurons (De Valois and Jacobs, 1968), and these become known as "adjectival" features. Thus, the structure of language, like the structure of perception, depends upon the structure of innate feature detectors in the brain. However, since perception involves both efferent and afferent processes, language also depends upon the maturational and individual historical reafferent effects of innately programmed efferent activities. Therefore, the structure of language reflects underlying structures in perceptual and motor systems, so that postulation of a separate brain structure that generates grammar in language appears unnecessary. Chomsky's (1968) syntactic analyses led him to conclude that there was a universal "deep structure" of language. The source of this deep structure is possibly best pursued through the analysis of perceptual processes. There is little reason to conclude that the perceptual systems of different races differ from one another to any great extent, and where physiological differences do exist, such as in sensitivity to different spectral wavelengths of visible light, then the language of color differs correspondingly (Bornstein, 1973).

Whereas Chomsky focuses on the syntax of language, Whorf (1956) concentrated on semantics and showed how different meanings in different languages reflected differences in cultural outlook. Whorf argued that language acts as a constraint on perception, because "through our mother tongue we are parties to an agreement to do so, not because nature itself is segmented in exactly that way for all to see."

Whorf emphasized the fact that the universe consists of more than can be discovered and described in our Indo-European language. But he appeared to believe that what is revealed in the consciousness of each individual culture is partial views of a whole "thing-in-itself" that constitutes external reality. He likened each culture's consciousness to individual searchlights that scan the whole universe but only reveal individual parts of it. He regarded, for example, biological evolutionary theory as an incomplete view, characteristic of the particular linguistic inheritance of Western culture. In Whorf's epistemology language is *prior to* knowledge. But in order to convince us that our knowledge of the world is limited by our Indo-European language,

Whorf must use an Indo-European language. Paradoxically, therefore, the very same reasons that he gives for devaluing biological evolutionary theory can be used to devalue his own theory of language. We find Whorf trapped in his own circle of thought—the inevitable fate of all deep thinkers. But although this circle has no escape, portions of it can become integral and necessary parts of other circles of thought, as I intend to show in the final chapter of this book.

Contrary to Whorf, my argument is that the study of language will not disclose external physical realities but instead will reveal the diversity of humanity's experience of the world. Whorf recognized that mathematical symbols and equations are specialized linguistic terms and form a continuous nexus with the other words used by a culture. Whorf's contention that electricity, for example, is "created" by the development of a suitable "word" that is expressed in special symbols and formulae is compatible with the present thesis that the subject matter of science is a biological product—the result of homeostatically related operations on the environment that bring into being new experiential phenomena that are then reified by being projected onto the external world. Whorf likened the scientific process to the construction of a figure from a background (in the same way that one can construe a form in a cloud). He cited the discovery of gravitation as an example.

Earlier I drew attention to Spengler's emphasis on the involvement of depth perception in the genesis of the different world views represented by each culture. The existence of each culture rests upon the prior existence of a visual experience of depth. Two concepts dominate the history of Western philosophy: space and time. The nature of reality has typically been expressed in terms of these two prime concepts, which when combined yield the concept of motion. Perception of space arose through the evolution of the oculomotor and visual processes; the perception of time arose through evolutionary interaction of the body with geophysical variations. The two perceptions together yield the experiences of motion, change, and causality. These experiences are then expressed in a language that is predominately visual—all scientific concepts or laws can be expressed in the form of a diagram of one sort or another.

Vision is the modality that dominates our experience, as is exemplified by experiments in which information from two modalities conflict. For example, Asch and Witkin (1948) found that when visual information is pitted against gravitational information conveyed by the vestibular and somatosensory systems, the visual information tends to predominate in its influence on the subject's behavior. However, it should be recognized that these results were obtained from city dwellers and may reflect their particular environments dominated by vertical and horizontal lines; in agrarian mountain-living communities somatosensory and vestibular information might have more impact on experience. If behavioral tests of perception of the vertical were performed on mountain goats, it is likely that gravitational information would predominate over visual information, especially since goats have poor spatial vision.

What I wish to emphasize here is that language rests upon a perceptual substratum. If biological and cultural evolution leads to modifications in the natural environment that alters its features, such as the construction of cities, then language must change accordingly. But since cultural evolution involves language and the effects of a culture influence its language, we are forced to recognize the existence of a circular process in the evolution of culture. Of course, our perceptions also depend upon the internal state of our bodies, so that they are influenced not only by the direct effects of environmental changes on our exteroceptive sense organs, but also by the effects of environmental changes on bodily homeostasis. For example, the current change from a positive to a negative connotation of the term "development" (of land) is undoubtedly in part a result of such adverse effects of crowded living on bodily homeostasis as air pollution.

Cultural alterations of the environment might even result in permanent physiological changes in perceptual processes, thereby affecting language development from within the brain itself. It was recently found in Canada that city dwellers of European descent have lower visual acuity for oblique lines (compared with horizontal and vertical lines) than do Cree Indian country dwellers (Annis and Frost, 1973). These differences were attributed to the tuning of orientation-specific detectors in the visual environment in early life, which for city dwellers is dominated by vertical and horizontal contours, but not for Cree Indians, whose tents and surrounding forests display contours in virtually all orientations. However, as the authors point out, an alternative explanation is also possible. The two populations may have genetic differences in the percentage of inherited oblique-line feature detectors, so that an orthogonal environment is created by those groups of people who possess fewer oblique-line feature detectors. Which of these alternatives is correct is not as important here as the point that the forms of language are interrelated with the evolution of the visual system.

New words are coined to describe mechanical inventions. But with the creation of inventions and the perception of their effects, earlier perceptions of nature are often reinterpreted relative to the man-made invention. The current tendency in neuroscience to view the nervous system as a kind of computer is a case in point. Prior to the invention of the computer the brain was likened to a telephone exchange, and prior to that to a hydraulic system. Attempts to explain human behavior and brain mechanisms by analogy with mechanical inventions inevitably results in another circle of thought, since the inventions themselves are outgrowths of human brain processes.

Whorf (1956) also discussed how so-called primitive cultures, such as the Hopi Indian, possess linguistic structures that are more suitable for the expression of concepts in contemporary physics than the structure of our Indo-European languages. Einsteinian relativity of space and time appears to be closer to the ordinary perceptions of a Hopi Indian than those of an educated person in an "advanced" Western culture. The Hopi Indian does not perceive time as a linear process and so does not objectify it by any measuring instrument. In fact, an equivalent word for time does not even exist in the Hopi language.

Whorf described how we in our Western culture have created an imaginary space in which mental events occur. That is, we assume that mental events must exist in a space of *some* kind since we assume that everything we know must reside somewhere within a four-dimensional space. By doing so, we have unwittingly created the Mind–Body problem, which has possessed the minds of philosophers since Aristotle. The reason for this mental torture is that by misconceiving Mind as existing in space, we then search for a *spatial* relation between Mind and Matter. Hopi Indians do not encounter this problem because they do not distinguish between thought and matter in the dualistic way that we do. They think that thought contacts everything and pervades the universe, much as we think light does. Whorf argues that "it is not unnatural to suppose that thought, like any other force, leaves everywhere traces of effect." Instead of thinking that thought goes out and engages with a rosebush, as the Hopi does, we think of our thought "dealing with a 'mental image' which is not the rosebush but a mental surrogate of it." Whorf raises the question, "Why should it be *natural* to think that our thought deals with a surrogate and not with the real rosebush?"

> Quite possibly because we are dimly aware that we carry about with us a whole imaginary space, full of mental surrogates. To us, mental surrogates are old familiar fare. Along with the images of imaginary space, which we perhaps secretly know to be only imaginary, we tuck the thought-of actually existing rosebush, which may be quite another story, perhaps just because we have that very convenient "place" for it. The Hopi thought-world has no imaginary space. The corollary to this is that it may not locate thought dealing with real space anywhere but in real space, nor insulate real space from the effects of thought. A Hopi would naturally suppose that his thought (or he himself) traffics with the actual rosebush—or more likely, corn plant—that he is thinking about. The thought then should leave some trace of itself with the plant in the field. If it is a good thought, one about health and growth, it is good for the plant; if a bad thought, the reverse.*

---

*Whorf, 1956, p. 150.

My reason for quoting from Whorf is not to try to convince the reader that the Hopi view of reality is closer to or further from the "truth" than that of Western science, but only that the duality of mind and body is by no means universal, and might very well be generated through the vagaries of our particular thought structures.

Let us consider the question of the location of thoughts, naively treating it as a meaningful question. Our perceptions seem to us to be located in the same spatial dimension as the physical events we believe cause them. When I look out into the world I see it extended in space beyond me, and not as images on some kind of screen inside my eye or head. When I touch an object with my finger I locate it at the end of my finger. When I touch it with a cane I locate it at the end of the cane.

As I already described, the experience of space is primarily dependent upon visual perception. The sense of space by touch is confined to the body and such artificial extensions as a cane. The degree to which the experience of space is generated by audition is unclear. Studies of blind people have not proved valuable in answering this question because our Indo-European description of the experience of space is predominately in visual terms. We do not possess linguistic terms with which to describe a space apprehended nonvisually. Von Senden's (1960) case studies of congenitally blind persons who were furnished sight by means of surgical operations late in their lives did not reveal the extent of pre-sight space perception in these individuals, since he himself did not examine the patients and language was employed by the ophthalmologists who did. A single more recent case study by Gregory and Wallace (1963) also used language to communicate with the patient about his perceptions. Although blind persons can correctly use words denoting spatial characteristics, this does not necessarily mean that they share the same experiences such words denote in sighted persons.

As Wittgenstein (1953, 1958) has shown, even in sighted people the same word in the same context can have widely varied meanings for various persons, and for the same person in different contexts. Nietszche (1880) anticipated Wittgenstein with his brief statement, "As if all words were not pockets into which now this and now that has been put, and now many things at once!" Heisenberg (1958) also realized that the meaning of a word cannot be defined absolutely through the use of other words:

> This intrinsic uncertainty of the meaning of words was of course recognized very early and has brought about the need for definitions, or—as the word "definition" says—for the setting of boundaries that determine where the word is to be used and where not. But definitions can be given only with the help of other concepts, and so one will finally have to rely on some concepts that are taken as they are, unanalyzed and undefined.

To comprehend the various meanings of a word we need to know all the occasions of its usage. Even were we able to do this, a word would have certain meanings only for a limited period in history, since usage continuously changes with time.

All that can safely be *stated* about the spatiality of the perceived world is that it consists of visually extended boundaries (in which are embedded auditory events) in coexistence with an internal spatial field of the body experienced through the somatosensory system. The visually experienced boundary of the body is correlated with much but not all of the somatosensorily experienced field of the body. Except by use of mirrors, photography, or television we are unable to visually perceive our back, face, neck, or the top of our head. Body movements that we see correspond with those that we feel, and the two together yield a unified experience of space.

Within the boundary set by the body's surface we experience a more poorly defined spatial field. Internal pains and rumblings of the stomach cannot be localized as precisely as can stimulation of the surface of the body. However, this imprecision in location of internal experiences is not entirely due to insufficient sensory innervation of the internal organs, but probably involves anatomic and motor limitations too. When asked to locate an itch on our skin we can usually point to it or touch it with relative precision. If it is on our back and inaccessible to touch, we then try to describe it, but consequently lose precision in doing so. But the ability to locate sensations of the body depends not only on their accessibility but also on familiarity and practice in doing so. For example, we can easily locate sensations in different parts of our mouth by using the tongue, but if we try to do so with our fingers, as in removing a fiber stuck between our teeth, we often fail on the first attempt and eventually have to use our tongue to guide the finger to the right spot.

The only area within the body that is devoid of sensation is the brain itself—a fact that seems to have escaped the attention of most neurophysiologists.* Even direct electrical stimulation of the brain does not yield any experience of the brain itself. Instead, motor

---

*Although headaches may be felt within the head, it is difficult to say exactly how far within—especially if the space occupied by the brain is never actually experienced as a referential locus.

activity, altered perceptions of the body or external
world, emotional feelings, and memories of earlier experiences are evoked, depending upon the locus of
stimulation. Destruction of nerve cells by an electrode
driven into the brain does not stimulate painful sensations in a patient, and therefore does not require the
administration of anesthetics to the brain. Even larger
injuries to the brain—whether from trauma or
disease—are not experienced as pain, but are manifested in alterations in other experiences and motor
functions. The "brain space," even if intruded upon, is
not itself experienced. We unconsciously carry about a
lucuna within our spatial world. This lacuna is not
unique, however, since we are not aware of the blind
spot in the visual field of each eye—corresponding to
the exit of the optic nerve from the retina—even though
it can be empirically demonstrated to "exist." Similarly,
persons who have suffered injury to the visual cortex
have lacunae within their visual fields of which they
have no conscious awareness under normal everyday
conditions.

What is the biological significance of this absence of
phenomenal experience within the brain? As I argued
earlier, body movements are functionally related to
survival—of the individual and of the species. The
brain is a specialized part of the body whose function is
to coordinate body movements. As I shall discuss later,
experiences are always associated with actual movements or with images of potential movements that
might serve to maintain homeostasis. Therefore, the potential adaptive value of conscious sensations of the
brain would lie in their association with manipulations
of the brain by the hands. Obviously, movements of this
kind would be unlikely to have any conceivable biolog-

ical adaptive functions because injury to the brain is irreversible. We experience pain because we are then able to alter our behavior adaptively, by not moving an injured ligament or fractured bone, by massaging the painful area, or by surgery. Since effective movements of the body depend upon the integrity of the brain, it also logically follows that an injured brain would not be likely to control effective movements of the hands to heal itself. For these reasons we can see why localization of a brain injury in experiential space has no adaptive value for movement, and why experiences of one's own brain have not evolved.

It does not make sense, therefore, to talk about sensations being located in the brain. We would not even know we had brains unless we studied other animal or human brains. Confusions arise whenever as observers of another individual's behavior, body, and brain we attempt to localize that individual's thoughts or mind spatially within his body or brain. Although we may discover, as observers, that certain brain or bodily events are necessary for what we call thinking, we should not identify those events with the thoughts themselves, as central-state materialists and identity theorists do. Although democratic institutions include an elected leader, we do not locate the dynamics of these institutions within the leader. Similarly, although stock exchanges and commodities markets may be central requirements for certain economic processes, we do not locate these economic processes in the markets or stock exchanges.

A somewhat closer analogy might be that of a battery and electricity. Although a battery can be considered a source of electricity, for the electricity to become manifest there must be a conducting medium connecting the two terminals of the battery. Electricity then pervades the entire system—including the connection—and is not located solely in the battery. Although we think of electricity being stored in the battery, this is only a metaphor. There is no way of "seeing" electricity in a disconnected battery.

We should regard consciousness in a similar manner. Metaphorically, the brain can be considered the source of consciousness (mind, thought, etc.), but consciousness only manifests itself through a brain existing in a physical environment. Consciousness must be thought of as pervading the brain *and those aspects of the environment with which the brain interacts.* It is an error to identify the brain as the source *and* locus of thought. Returning to the analogy of electricity, once we connect the two battery terminals with a conductive wire we can measure the presence of electricity anywhere within the wire or battery, i.e., electricity appears within and flows throughout the whole system. It is the same with the evolution of the brain—consciousness is the result of the interaction of the evolving brain and the evolving environment.

Electricity will not be manifested anywhere if all we have is loose wires and disconnected batteries lying around. Similarly, if one could conceivably deafferentate a newborn infant's entire brain (including its interocepters), while maintaining the organism's viability, it would be difficult to imagine that infant experiencing anything without differential patterns of activity being generated within the brain as a result of afferent or reafferent processes. Thoughts originate from perceptions, and there is no possibility they can be localized in any space other than that which is the perceptual experience itself—which is to say they have no *locus* at all.

The mind–body problem, according to which certain independently obtained conclusions about the world appear to be mutually contradictory, represents an intellectual confusion peculiar to Western thought. The crux of the problem lies in the concept of space and the idea that thoughts can be located within space. It stems from the Cartesian dualistic notion that the world is constituted of mind and matter, with mind interacting with matter at the pineal gland in the brain. Although Descartes' suggestion that the pineal gland was the locus of interaction between mind and body has been disclaimed, mind–body interactionists continue to believe that thoughts influence physiological brain processes *somewhere* within the brain, such as the cerebral cortex (e.g., Eccles, 1970; Sperry, 1969), in contrast to the Hopi or East Indians, who think of thoughts as pervading the universe. Even most Western central-state materialists, identity theorists, or psychophysical parallelists think of thoughts as having spatial location within the brain.* Some Western philosophers who do not share the view that the locus of thoughts is in the brain have proposed extra dimensions of space unique to mental events (e.g., Price, 1953; Smythies, 1965). Overall, however, most Western philosophers consider thoughts to be situated in some space or other. Because consciousness is dependent upon the integrity of the brain does not necessarily mean that consciousness is spatially located there. The brain is the portal of consciousness, not its container.

---

*Identity theorists hold that mentalistic and physicalistic expressions refer to one and the same thing, namely *physical* phenomena, in the same way that the word "water" and the expression H_2O denote an identical thing. Central state materialists go a step further and identify the mental phenomena with events in the central nervous system. Psychophysical parallelists believe mental and physical events are merely correlated, without any causal connection.

Toulmin (1972) has also attributed part of the intellectual confusion surrounding the mind–body problem to the restricted application of cognitive terms to the brain, rather than to the functional interaction of entire human beings with an environment.

> . . . it cannot help being as much of an oversimplification to talk of a man's *brain* as "thinking" or "acquiring knowledge" in isolation—apart from the external problems or situations *towards which* that thought or knowledge is directed—as it is to talk of a biochemical reaction as "adaptive" in isolation, without making explicit the particular environment—including the particular evolutionary competitors—*to which* that "adaptation" is relative. Our "mental" categories are given their literal meaning—and so are literally intelligible—in relation to the lives and activities of entire human beings, and then can be applied to particular parts of humans (even their brains) only in a transferred, metaphorical sense. Most particularly, our "cognitive" terms are given their literal meaning in relation to the *success* or *failure* of entire human beings in dealing with the tasks they encounter. Now, of course, no brain structure or brain process could meaningfully be described as "successful" or "unsuccessful," *tout pur*, regardless of the external task in terms of which "success" and "failure" are defined; any more than an organism can be "adapted" in some absolute sense, regardless of the environment and competitors with which it has to deal. Just as no biochemical reaction is *intrinsically* "adaptive," so no physiological or psychological process is intrinsically "cognitive."

It should be clear by now that the mind–body problem involves a confusion *in cognition* of the relationship between "mind" and "space," and is not simply a confusion in the use of language. The confusion must necessarily be expressed in language, but language is not the cause of the confusion. Wittgenstein was aware of this. Although he is often misrepresented as a major figure in the modern linguistic school of philosophers, Wittgenstein believed the task of philosophy was to clear up the confusions that *appear* to be created by language, but which in reality are cognitive inconsistencies perpetuated through "language games." Unfortunately, we are constrained in dealing with these confusions by the ambiguity of language itself.

Because "mind," "consciousness," and "thoughts" are not localizable in space, the question of causal action by the mind upon the body, or the body upon the mind cannot arise, since causality involves necessary relations between events occurring in local systems. However, certain relations between mental and physical phenomena do not involve any limitations in space or time, but can be related at widely different points in both space and time. In other words, the related phenomena need not be conjoined in space and time. In order to deal with these phenomena, Jung (1960c) developed the concept of "synchronicity." He proposed that events in the universe were related by principles involving either causality or synchronicity.

Causality has been a subject of considerable philosophical debate. I shall regard it in the same way as Hume did, as a property of the mind, but one that derives from certain underlying psychological principles. Hume (1888) argued that "We have no other notion of cause and effect, but that of certain objects which have been *always conjoined* together. . . . We cannot penetrate into the reason of the conjunction." With the addition of an empirical stipulation, we can bring Hume's definition up to date. An event can be considered to cause another if both are uniquely and invariably correspondent in space and time, and if one fails to occur, the other also fails to occur. The distinction between causality and correlation rests on the latter proviso. Correlations are frequently observed between two events (especially in the social sciences), but if either of the events continues to occur in the absence of the other, neither event can be said to cause the other.

What about events that are correlated but at different loci in space and time, and still the removal of one leads to the nonoccurrence of the other—are those events not causally related? It is generally considered that they are, but not in a direct manner. It is assumed that A is linked to B through a chain of *intermediate* causally related events. Are these not cases of synchronicity? The answer is no. Synchronistic events are as much separated in four-dimensional space as are correlated events, but they differ qualitatively from correlated and causally related events. This qualitative distinction between correlated and synchronistic events is psychobiological, and has nothing to do with quantitative aspects of space and time, as is commonly believed.

Correlated events are intuitively regarded as distinct events and not as a single event extended in space or time. A chair, for example, is usually considered to be a single event and not a series of correlated events synchronous in time and extended in space. The collision of two balls is considered a causally related event involving the first ball arriving at conjunctive points in space and time with the second ball. The motion of the first or (subsequently) the second ball is not usually reduced to a series of intermediate causally connected events (although it can be, as in statistical mechanics). The cause of the first ball's rolling is attributed to some change in the environment of the first ball, such as the movement of an object towards it (a finger or a magnet).

Synchronistic phenomena, by contrast, are identified with experiences that are considered to be "nonphysical" but qualitatively identical with other experiences considered to be physical. The nonphysical aspect involves imagination as opposed to sensation and perception, i.e., it is extrasensory.* When a psychic experiences an image or "vision" of physical events that another person perceives directly, their phenomenal descriptions concur; but an independent scientist would not be able to correlate the description of the psychic with a series of causally related events involving both the physical environment and the psychic's nervous system as he could for the other person.† In the case of

---

*But it should be recognized that the term "extrasensory" could be inaccurate. If the physical events envisioned by the psychic could be causally related to physiological events in the psychic's nervous system, through the development of novel instruments and techniques, then a new sensory modality would be discovered and ESP would fall into the conventional framework of psychophysics. Since extrasensory phenomena are relatively elusive, it is also possible that problems in their measurement may be similar to those in quantum mechanics. If the physical energy levels involved in ESP are extremely low, then the energy exchange involved in their measurement by instruments might be so great as to render them unmeasurable. In this case we would never be in a position to empirically establish extrasensory phenomena as conventional psychophysical phenomena. Another possibility is that ESP involves interaction between signals emitted by the brain and the environment, similar to echolocation (as in bats) or electrolocation (as in electric fish). If the brain of the experimenter affects the energy exchanges between the subject's brain and the external events, especially under conditions in which the experimenter has a "negative attitude" toward ESP, then the common failure to confirm the positive findings of favorably disposed experimenters would make sense. Given the present state of knowledge and experimental sophistication of this field, it is impossible to evaluate the relative probabilities of these various possibilities.

†The empirical investigations published in the parapsychological literature are as rigorous (and in many cases more so) in their experimental and analytic methods as those published in the psychological and biological literature. Because one set of findings does not fit into a preestablished intellectual framework as readily as another set does not warrant their rejection. The same criticisms of methodology and statistical analysis aimed at the parapsychological literature apply equally to the psychological literature. Unconscious motivation to obtain results consistent with hypotheses, as has been demonstrated to occur in psychological investigations (Rosenthal, 1966), is probably equal in both fields.

precognition, although the phenomenal descriptions of the psychic and the other person concur, they do not coincide in time.

Since there is a close or even complete correspondence between the psychic's image and the perceived event, one of them cannot be said to cause the other in any conventional sense of the word "cause." To do so would be analogous to saying that the event of a pendulum at a certain point in space and time was the cause of the next occasion at which the pendulum was at that same point in space. If we recognize that our concept of cause is unique to our Western scientific world view, as pointed out by Spengler and Whorf, then we can see that causality and synchronicity represent different modalities of the brain rather than intrinsic differences in "physical" phenomena.

Either successive images of physical events can be perceived as resulting from certain discontinuities in energy flow, or images of physical events occur "spontaneously" without any causal antecedents. The first type of perception constitutes causality, the second synchronicity. The two perceptions need not be contradictory, since the events whose images are experienced synchronistically by one person may be experienced causally by another either because the latter employs scientific instruments or the vantage points of the persons differ in space and time. Thus, synchronicity is more akin to the intuitive than with the analytic sense, and allied with wisdom rather than with knowledge. The opposition between causality and synchronicity may be compared to that of Western science and Eastern mysticism.

Synchronicity and causality differ in that causality can only be established by empirical methods whereas synchronicity can be made manifest incidentally as well as experimentally. Furthermore, causal perception can be used to guide action in the world according to scientifically formulated general laws of nature, whereas synchronistic perception cannot. Causality applies to the general, whereas synchronicity applies to the specific; that is, causality demands the explanation and prediction of regular events in the universe, whereas synchronicity demands the perception and prediction of a specific incident. Although the two forms of perception are not mutually contradictory, they are mutually exclusive. Synchronicity involves the prediction of events that cannot be predicted according to established natural laws. In this way the two perceptions constitute complementary mental perspectives. Of course, the ultimate aim of causal analysis, as epitomized in science, is to incorporate all synchronistic events within it and thereby eliminate the particular. This would represent a completely mechanistic interpretation of the universe, in which all phenomena resulted from necessity according to the principles of general laws. There has been endless discussion of the validity of materialistic interpretations of natural phenomena, which I shall consider later; but I wish to emphasize here my contention that the aim of inclusiveness of materialism is a vain one and that the two perceptual perspectives represent complementary rather than contradictory viewpoints of natural phenomena.

Jung specifically proposed that synchronicity depends on the archetypes in the Collective Unconscious. I described earlier how an organism need only experience a single environmental event for its inherited cyclic activity patterns to become synchronized with cyclic alterations in environmental conditions. Perhaps such behaviors represent crude prototypes of the complex kinds of synchronistic perceptions that Jung described, in that a primitive organism alters its behavior in preparation for a future event without understanding the causes of its own behavior. In a sense this process is built into the genes of the organism so as to ensure the appearance of behaviors synchronous with environmental changes, but need not manifest itself at the intellectual level. Instead, the intellect is concerned with formulating phenomenal regularities that, as a result of human evolution, are not intuited. Thus, causality depends on learning, whereas synchronicity depends on instinct and intuition.

Synchronicity, correlation, and causality represent different modes of perception of external physical events. Hallucinations and images differ from these modes by depending solely on internal events, not bearing any necessary relation to external events. But hallucinations are indistinguishable in experience from perceptions and are therefore considered to be real, whereas images are not. What is the phenomenal distinction between an image and a hallucination? That is to say, what is it that makes an hallucination seem real? It is its consistent unity with all other aspects of ongoing experience. Imagination usually involves activity that in some way divorces a person from the context of his environment. For example, a visual image superimposed upon the surrounding perceptual field may cause the latter to recede in prominence. Such acts as defocusing or closing one's eyes, stopping one's ears, leaning back in a chair and staring at a uniform surface such as a ceiling typically accompany imagination. These acts remove attention from the exterior to the interior. These attentional acts also evoke reafferent activity by which the resulting images are recognized to be images rather than hallucinations. Experiential relations between images also contribute to the distinction, since any seeming incongruity between one image and the next leads to a questioning of their reality. Lack of congruity between successive experiences creates images rather than hallucinations.

The "phantom limb" phenomenon can illustrate this difference. Patients who have had a limb amputated sometimes continue to feel as though the limb were still intact. This experience can vary from imagination to hallucination depending upon the context in which it appears. If the patient is sitting still quietly with eyes closed, there is nothing in his or her experience that is inconsistent with the experience of the phantom limb except the memory that the limb was severed. Whenever this memory is temporarily forgotten the phantom limb is experienced as a hallucination, and whenever the memory of the accident or surgery returns the experience turns into one of imagination. Of course, if the patient opens his eyes or becomes active he will experience the phantom limb as imagination (illusion); that is, inconsistencies within phenomenal experience will show the experience to be an illusion. The absence of appropriate reafferent activity from proprioceptors or the failure of the imagined limb to make contact with external objects will generate inconsistencies in phenomenal experience; so does attempting to feel the phantom limb with another part of the body, either by moving another bodily part into the expected space of the phantom limb or by moving the phantom limb into the actual space of some part of the body.

By contrast, hallucinations are not recognized as such by psychiatric patients, who act as though they were real; that is, no inconsistencies within their experiences are recognized. Hearing voices when a faucet is turned on, believing the drinking water has been poisoned so that it induces nausea, or believing other persons to be hostile all fit comfortably into the internally consistent pattern of experience of schizophrenics.

The distinction between what is regarded as a hallucination by one person and reality by another is one of logic. Laing (1967), Szasz (1961), and others have concluded that the definition of hallucination, delusion, and schizophrenia depends to some extent upon the cultural context in which it occurs. Such anthropologists as La Barre (1954), Benedict (1959), and Whorf have contributed to the development of this viewpoint by emphasizing that patterns of behavior considered entirely normal within one culture might be considered schizophrenic were they to occur in another culture. In theory, the presence of a hallucination in one person can be empirically demonstrated by another person by means of suitable instruments for measuring brain activity, which would show that the physically measurable brain events do not correlate with physically measurable events in the external world. In practice, however, the idea of carrying out such an empirical verification itself arises because of differences in experience between the schizophrenic and the scientist (cf. Laing, 1967). The scientific behavior and its associated conceptual system of beliefs might very well be considered "schizophrenic" by members of other cultures. One can never escape from this relativistic web of human experience. All that we can do is refine our cultural-conceptual system of thought so as to eliminate as many inconsistencies within its internal logic as possible.

Pathological hallucinations indicate that brain events are sufficient in themselves to evoke experiences. But they are only sufficient in a *historical context,* having been built up as an accumulation of past experiences that involved more than the brain alone. As discussed earlier, perceptions and memory depend upon reafferent activity evoked by bodily interactions with the environment. In the absence of this history of interactions, brain events in themselves would not be sufficient to generate any meaningful experiences *as we know them.* In other words, they do not occur *de novo* but are based on a pattern of events occurring both externally and internally within the body and brain. Once established, brain events can become independent of their origins, thereby creating experiences in the absence of external events. Hypothetically, internal rearrangements of brain events could possibly occur in a brain isolated from the environment, but these would still stem from a phylogenetic history of interaction between organism and environment.

7   Will

I now wish to consider the relationship between patterns of efferent activity resulting in bodily movements and the experiences that precede and accompany them. This relationship will bear on the traditional question of free will and determinism.

The feeling of volition or will arises directly from within us and is not inferred from perceptions of external events. If we ourselves did not feel volition in performing acts, i.e., that we will them, it would be difficult to imagine, on the basis of observation of behavior alone, that such feelings might exist in other organisms. This feeling of volition is often projected onto inanimate moving objects as well as onto other animals. The motions of the planets, for example, are explained in some cultures as manifestations of the wills of various gods. In Western materialistic philosophies, such as

those of Descartes and Leibniz, the deterministic structure of natural events ultimately rests on the will of
God. Even in modern science some scientists attribute
their discoveries of order in universal events to the will
of God, as did Newton. The same tendency exists in
young children, who often attribute the motions of inanimate objects to the will of an agency such as the
wind, or even to a will within the object itself—so that a
ball rolls in a particular way "because it wants to."

The problem of will today is no longer merely a
philosophical exercise. It has taken on new dimensions
in the conflict between our feeling that our behavior is
directed by the will and the results of empirical investigations that indicate that behavior is determined. Even
in determinists the intellectual belief that behavior is
physically determined does not eliminate feelings of
volition. It is as if this belief applied to the behavior of
others but not to the believer. Paradoxically, it is especially when our intellect is suspended and we are en-
gulfed in strong emotions, such as anger or fear, that the
feeling of will deserts us and we tend to act in ways that
seem "out of our hands." At such times it is as though
more powerful forces take over control of our actions.
When asked to explain our behavior we might say something like "I didn't know what I was doing." The absence of the feeling of will is therefore not necessarily a
result of intellectual knowledge.

Of course, it may be premature to accept the claim
that our behavior is entirely determined by a physical
mechanistic process that, given time and patience, will
be completely elucidated at various levels of scientific
analysis. Since the empirical evidence is not yet in,
judgement on the whole question can be suspended on
this basis alone. But there are logical reasons why

complete empirical data will never exist. I have already alluded to some of these reasons in discussing reinforcement. It is logically impossible for humans to construct any system of physical laws that can completely embrace an *evolving* nature, since the system would have to explain the human behavior responsible for the formulation of the system. It is difficult to conceive how the novelty of human behavior alone (including the development of science itself) could be predicted on the basis of natural laws. These objections to determinism of human behavior have already been forcefully stated by Bergson and Spengler, among others, and are difficult to counter.

Cartesian mathematics proved to be an effective method for the representation of motion and led to the development of differential calculus and Newtonian mechanics. Newtonian mechanics paved the way for the industrial revolution, with its generally adaptive effects. As a result, our interaction with nature has become more effective. The biological value of the intellect, as exemplified by the rise of modern science, lies in the adaptive function of effective action on the environment. In view of the successful application of scientific laws to inanimate matter, it was hoped that the same deterministic laws might also apply to organic nature, including whole organisms and the physiological events that underlie behaviors directly associated with our experience of the will. It is often claimed that if such application of determinism to humans should prove to be successful, then the feeling of will must be an illusion. However, in this chapter I shall argue that this claim is not valid and that the idea of the will and determinism represent two different and nonconflicting perspectives of experience accompanying two distinct roles of the individual in society. In order to do so let me first consider the phenomenology of the will.

Bergson (1937) associates the will with conscious actions of choice. He points out that as behavior proceeds along a given path directed by instinct, there is little consciousness of that behavior. However, if an instinctual act is in some way thwarted, then consciousness comes to the fore—the possibility of alternate actions is made apparent and a choice must be made. In this way, Bergson identifies the intellect with conscious choice, and therefore indirectly with the will. This identification is consistent with the association I drew a little earlier between the presence of strong emotion and suspension of the will. In Bergson's system, consciousness is present whenever ongoing mechanistically determined behaviors are impeded.

Once a novel behavior that achieves the aim of the thwarted instinctual behavior is selected, then that behavior is reinforced and is likely to occur the next time the same instinctual behavior is thwarted. Eventually the learned behavior supersedes the instinctual behavior and becomes a habit. This situation is especially prone to develop during early infancy, when behavior is largely governed by instinct. Similarly, once an assembly of habits has been acquired, then when any one of these habits is thwarted, new consciously learned alternative acts emerge to take their place.

Bergson used the word "consciousness" somewhat restrictively, confining it to feelings of will. But, as I have already indicated, consciousness includes much more than feelings of will. The will does not pervade the whole of consciousness, but represents an aspect of consciousness that only emerges when instincts or habits are thwarted. Bearing this in mind and substituting "will" for "consciousness" in the following quotation from Bergson (1937: 159–160), we obtain an illuminating description of the genesis of the will.

When we mechanically perform an habitual action, when the somnambulist automatically acts his dream, unconsciousness may be absolute, but this is merely due to the fact that the representation of the act is held in check by the performance of the act itself, which resembles the idea so perfectly, and fits it so exactly, that consciousness is unable to find room between them. *Representation is stopped up by the action.* The proof of this is, that if the accomplishment of the act is arrested or thwarted by an obstacle, consciousness may reappear. It was there, but neutralized by the action which fulfilled and thereby filled the representation. The obstacle creates nothing positive; it simply makes a void, removes a stopper. This inadequacy of act to representation is precisely what we here call consciousness.

If we examine this point more closely, we shall find that consciousness is the light that plays around the zone of possible actions or potential activity which surrounds the action really performed by the living being. It signifies hesitation or choice. Where many equally possible actions are indicated without there being any real action (as in a deliberation that has not come to an end), consciousness is intense. Where the action performed is the only action possible (as in activity of the somnambulistic or more generally automatic kind), consciousness is reduced to nothing. Representation and knowledge exist none the less in the case if we find a whole series of systemized movements the last of which is already prefigured in the first, and if, besides, consciousness can flash out of them at the shock of an obstacle. From this point of view, the *consciousness of a living being may be defined as an arithmetical difference between potential and real activity. It measures the interval between representation and action.*

The will is associated with the "arrest" of instinctual behaviors and habits directed toward the maintenance of homeostatic rhythms. In other words, the will tends to be associated with what might be called economic or utilitarian types of behavior. In the kinds of situations in which the will arises, as described by Bergson, a particular goal comes to mind as a "representation" and a choice is made among a variety of potential acts in an attempt to achieve that representation. The representation is present in consciousness before the willed act is performed. By contrast, there is no clear representation as such accompanying the most highly creative acts (whether that of scientist or artist), which emerge spontaneously without a person feeling any direct involvement of the will or choice in the act of creation. The creation arises internally in an unimpelled manner. In fact, to refer to a "creative act" is really a contradiction in terms, since we tend to think of an *act* as behavior directed towards the fulfillment of a goal or representation already in mind, particularly when the verb "to act" is used in the sense "to fill a role."

In accord with Bergson, I shall consider the will to be linked with acts *on objects* and designed to have the effect of fulfilling a representation or goal. All of these willed acts proceed outward from the body toward objects in space surrounding the body. The will is concerned with the bringing about of certain events. It is in this sense that Nietzsche (1968) conceived the "will to power" as an overcoming or achieving. Once willed acts have achieved their aim they become automatized and are incorporated into the general repertory of behavior and are performed unconsciously. The will is not in conflict with its product—unconsciousness. In fact, I shall argue later that it is only through the will that the concepts of automatism and unconsciousness, considered to be characteristic of a deterministic process, came into being.

Because the will is associated with acts means that it is also associated with patterns of efferent activity. This is a truism, of course, but it should be emphasized that patterns of efferent activity do not necessarily bring about bodily movement. Will and intention involve a sense of *possible* or potential efforts to bring about certain states of affairs. These efforts need not be restricted to bodily movements, but can use technological means to produce movement of objects. Even sheer brain activity can alter physical conditions outside the body, as in "biofeedback" situations, where selected patterns of EEG activity may be used to move a galvanometer or loudspeaker.* Therefore, the will is associated with patterns of efferent activity having the potential of generating movements of the body in space. So an understanding of the will involves us once more in considerations of *space*.

Earlier, I described how the perception of space depends upon physical action. The experience of space depends as much upon the existence of patterns of efferent activity as it does on patterns of afferent activity. A spatial world constructed purely of perceptual aspects of boundaries of brightness and color is inconceivable

---

*However, it has not been unequivocally demonstrated that in these "biofeedback" situations there is no pattern of covert skeletal muscular activity associated with the altered patterns of brain activity. Parapsychologists might claim that will extends to psychokinesis (PK), where the behavior of such objects as dice or electronic random-number-generators are assumed to be directly influenced by thoughts without any known intervening physical forces being exerted upon them. But even if the experimental results upon which claims for the existence of PK are based are found to be valid, the phenomena itself can equally well be reduced to one of synchronicity. PK and synchronicity cannot be distinguished from one another by experiment, since successes could represent precognition of future events rather than the will actually influencing the events themselves.

without these perceptual aspects being related to actions that can affect them. Ancient estimates of the extension of space were extremely small. Cosmic space was thought to be limited, a view that was undoubtedly based upon the limited abilities of ancient astronomers to "act on celestial phenomena" by means of measurement. Space today is considered infinite in its extent—the direct result of our ability to measure spatial distances in terms of light years—and is represented in the fourth dimension of time. We think of space in terms of the trajectory of a point of light, upon which we imagine ourselves riding through the dimension of time. This image is derived from the first movements we make as babies when reaching for objects. As a result of these movements, afferent visual activity alters in concordance with patterns of efferent activity, and the conjunction of the two patterns yields an experience of space. Only later in development do visual aspects of the experience become separated from intentional acts so that we forget how they developed.

Since the experience of will involves action in space, the experiences of will and space are intertwined. In early infancy, when behavior is mainly instinctive, the experience of will is probably largely absent. As the infant learns to grasp surrounding objects, space extends outward from its body and feelings of will find their place within space.

As Wittgenstein (1953) pointed out in a discussion on willing, when our fingers are crossed a certain way we are usually unable to move a particular finger someone points to—if he "merely shows it to the eye. If on the other hand he touches it, we can move it." This example illustrates the importance of space in our feelings of will. Unless we have a schema of bodily movement that

corresponds to a visual schema of space, we are unable
to will movements in correspondence with the visual
schema. In my earlier discussion of disarranged perception (and Festinger's experiments in particular), I
concluded that efferent activity is usually reorganized
relative to visual afferent activity. This is also the case
in the example of crossed fingers, where the sensorimotor schema is spatially disarranged relative to the
visual field. Since the will is identified with an action
directed in a visually defined space, unless the body as
visually perceived corresponds with the body perceived sensorimotorly, the will cannot exert itself in
action. The willed act—moving a particular finger identified visually—cannot occur. Practice is required to
rearrange the sensorimotor schema of the disarranged
fingers relative to the visual schema before the will can
exert itself again.

Because feelings of will express themselves through
acts in space, it does not follow that the will causes
behavior. The question of whether the will causes behavior is meaningless, since in a deterministic system
the will would have to exist in identifiable loci in space
to affect the physical matter of the brain. As I have already argued, this possibility does not exist for
consciousness—there cannot be any interaction between consciousness and matter.

The example of the crossed fingers also points up the
implication of expectation in the use of the word "will."
If a willed act does not occur as expected because our
body encounters some obstacle, then we say our will
was *impeded*. On the other hand, if a willed (expected)
effect does not occur because of a disarrangement of our
sensorimotor schema, as above, then we experience the
peculiar feeling of being unable to exert our will—as

though the will knows what to do but somehow cannot grasp hold of the right act. The will and the act are thus identified with each other. Wittgenstein (1955) made the same identification.

> Willing, if it is not to be a sort of wishing, must be the action itself. It cannot be allowed to stop anywhere short of the action. If it is the action, then it is so in the ordinary sense of the word; so it is speaking, writing, walking, lifting a thing, imagining something. But it is also trying, attempting, making an effort—to speak, to write, to lift a thing, to imagine something, etc.
>
> I raise my arm, I have *not* wished it might go up. The voluntary action excludes this wish. It is indeed possible to say: "I hope I shall draw the circle faultlessly." And that is to express a wish that one's hand should move in such-and-such a way.

Here Wittgenstein brings out the distinction between willing and wishing. Wishing represents a feeling that certain actions might cause certain events to happen, but an uncertainty exists as to which specific actions might be effective. Willing involves knowledge acquired by past experience—of how to bring about certain effects by certain actions. Thus, in contrast to wishing, willing involves confirming—the actualization of expectation.

The moment an instinctual behavior or habit does not achieve its usual ends, a feeling of consternation arises and the environment is surveyed to try to identify and overcome the perceived cause of the disruption. A new or altered habit may result, and the original habit disappears by a process called "extinction." Thus, reinforcement of a willed novel act through the occurrence of certain anticipated patterns of reafferent activity is similar to the kind of reinforcement involved in predictive learning in that the anticipated reafferent patterns are the equivalent of feature detectors. Bergson's definition of the will "as an arithmetical difference between potential and real activity" may thus be restated as follows: the will exists to the degree an instinctual or learned act does not bring about certain patterns of reafferent activity. This reformulation brings out the association of reinforcement and will in the acquisition of new acts. Reinforcement occurs to the degree that a representation (in neural terms, a pattern of reafferent activity) is achieved by a novel behavior. The representation disappears completely from consciousness when a habit is acquired. The will then lies latent within the habit and only emerges (with the representation) if the habit should fail to achieve its usual end.

If a person is presented with two alternatives for possible action, what kinds of experience does he undergo in making a choice between them? Imagine a situation involving the relatively simple choice of whether to eat an apple or a banana. The characteristics of each fruit might be important. Is the apple hard and smooth? Does the banana have brown spots? Associations may be ushered in of wrinkled apples not being crisp or of bananas with brown spots having soggy centers. Memories of previous occasions on which each fruit was eaten might flash through the person's mind and reevoke feelings of pleasantness or unpleasantness according to the circumstances. It is very likely that if the person lingers over the choice, several images will pass through his or her mind. Choice is finally based upon the relative affective tone of the two different sets of memories and can be said to consist of vicarious pleasures and displeasures. Since the constellations of memories are accompanied by fragments of the patterns of autonomic activity that occurred at the time of the remembered experiences, the action taken will depend on the relative affective qualities of the patterns of autonomic activity evoked by each image. The experiences of images and autonomic activation constitute the experiential feelings characteristic of will and its exercise as choice.

Since willing is associated with expectancies based on past experiences of reinforcement, it should be accessible to experimental analysis. Although there has been relatively little psychophysiological research on expectancy in animals, some recent investigations by Levine, Goldman, and Coover (1973) represent a significant step in this direction. In one experiment two groups of thirsty rats were trained to press a lever to obtain water, using a fixed interval (FI) schedule of reinforcement for one group, and a variable interval (VI) schedule for the other. The schedules were set so that the amount of reinforcement that each group obtained over a given interval of time was the same. Subsequently, it was observed that levels of the "stress" hormone, adrenocorticotrophic hormone (ACTH) rose markedly when the group trained on the FI schedule was shifted to the VI schedule, but not when the group trained on the VI schedule was shifted to the FI schedule. If the rats had acquired a memory of the temporal pattern of reinforcement, then they would have an expectancy of reinforcement occurring at certain regular times in the FI condition, but no particular temporal expectancy of reinforcement in the VI schedule. Therefore, it appears reasonable to infer from these results that the rats had both memory and expectancy of the pattern of reinforcement in the FI conditions and that the sharp rise in output of ACTH reflected the disappointment of not receiving expected reinforcements when shifted from FI to VI schedules.

The behaviorist might argue that we have no reason to infer the existence of memory, expectancy, or disappointment in a rat since its behavior is determined in a mechanical way in these and other experiments, and that it adds nothing to the value of behavioral science to introduce mentalist language into the description of events. But what the behaviorist does not recognize is that he is guilty of unwittingly importing this same mentalist language into his experiments.

Clearly, the idea for an experiment such as the foregoing arises in the first place because of the experiences of expectancy and disappointment we humans feel under similar circumstances. Before people become professional psychologists they experience many feelings and emotions that they do not analyze. Later on they may become interested in such analysis and as a result become psychologists. Psychology evolved in order to understand these experiences and therefore owes its own existence to them. When a psychologist is studying humans it is legitimate to retain the usage of mental terms such as "expectancy," "frustration," or "disappointment" because we assume these terms refer to feelings universal to humanity, otherwise a language denoting their existence could not have evolved. But the behaviorist argues that since we do not share a common language with animals we are not justified in imputing to animals the existence of experiences akin to our own.

There appear to be two logical paradoxes in this argument. First, one purpose of animal investigations is to cast light on our own experiences and behavior. The fact that we represent one branch of an evolutionary tree whose historical trunk we share with all other animals constitutes a sound reason for carrying out comparative studies on animals to determine the degree to which they share with us common anatomical, physiological, and behavioral patterns. If behaviorists argue that experiences are epiphenomena that merely accompany physically determined processes of behavior, this is not a sound reason for denying the existence of similar epiphenomena in a species of animal that shares the same behavioral patterns with humans. Second, the design of animal experiments is derived from the experiences of humans, which, it is hoped, will be clarified by the results of the animal experiments. Psychologists typically analyze the conditions under which particular phenomena arise in their own experience and then try to construct the same conditions for animals. They intuitively understand the kinds of environmental contingencies that bring out, for example, the feeling of expectation, and then create the same contingencies for animal subjects to determine whether these contingencies produce the same kinds of behavior in the experimental animals as they do in themselves. If successful in this venture, an animal model of a human process is claimed. The model then allows investigations into the physiological events accompanying the behavior. If for ethical reasons these investigations are not possible directly in humans, they are performed on animal subjects. But it is assumed that similar physiological events are also present in humans and that these determine the behavior with which the experience arises as an epiphenomenon.

The behaviorist might argue further that the mental experiences are *merely* epiphenomena and are not involved in the generation of the environmental contingencies surrounding the animal subjects. If this is the case, then the mental experiences of the behaviorist himself must likewise be epiphenomena accompanying that behavioral expression, and are not involved in the generation of his argument. But if this is so, how is language generated? Are words no more than vibratory patterns in the body or air? We find ourselves confronted by the kind of "mental cramp" that Wittgenstein described when we pursue this kind of argument. It can usually be traced to the misuse of language. In this particular case, we know intuitively that conscious experience *is involved* in the generation of language. We experience this knowledge as an indubitable internal fact. We use language to express our thoughts and intentions and influence the behavior of others.

A behaviorist observing two people communicating verbally with one another can describe language in terms of mathematical functions and diagrams of physical events in the environment and in their bodies and brains so as to effectively determine their verbal behavior. But we must recognize, as Whorf did, that the mathematical formulas and diagrams are specialized "words" too, which originated in order to communicate the mutual experiences of scientists. Therefore, the behaviorist's consciousness lurks behind the mathematically described "physical" events that he supposes exclusively determine behavior. Now the behaviorist's mathematical language itself demands a physical explanation that can only be proffered by a second behaviorist, and so on *ad infinitum*. Consciousness can never be entirely removed from the picture, however hard behaviorists may try to evade it. There is no good reason against inferring the existence of similar conscious experiences in animals as in humans, if both share similar patterns of behavior, anatomy, and physiology. It is self-contradictory to attribute the principal uniqueness of man to his consciousness and language, and yet deny its part in certain behaviors with which it is uniquely associated, because those behaviors appear to be mechanistically determined in animal experiments. An approach of this kind represents a denial of the importance of consciousness in the intellectual processes of the scientist, through which the data of determinism are themselves yielded.

The conscious experiences of the observer and experimental subject are potentially interchangeable. If they were not, scientific method would break down when applied to psychology. If the experimenter were unable to imagine the experiences of the subject because they did not share any common experience, he would not have a psychology of the subject to study.

Imagine trying to perform a psychological experiment on consciousness (as opposed to behavior) in a culture whose language one did not understand. The first requirement would be to learn the language so that one could enter into the consciousness of the alien culture. Wittgenstein (1958) described how the meaning of language (which is what one actually learns) is the context of behavior, for which words stand as symbols. If the physical environment and social structure of an alien culture were *totally* different in every respect from the culture in which the observer was raised, it would be extremely difficult for him to grasp the meaning of the foreign language. There are always subtle nuances in the meanings of words that are unique to the language of a particular culture and which can never be completely grasped by a foreigner who has not learned the language in the same behavioral contexts as the native speaker. Of course, because of the universal structure of the human brain, and the limitations on variation in the global physical environment, there are common structures in existential experience that are universal to humans. There are therefore certain universal meanings in all languages.

Two different aspects of experience must be reconciled—that of the subject in an experiment and that of the observer. The behavior of the subject may appear determined to the observer, but only as a result of the experimental procedures designed through the will of the observer. When we are in the role of a subject in an experiment we are not able to view our *own* willed behavior as determined in the way the observer can. Therefore, the experiences of free will and determinism of ones own behavior cannot occur simultaneously. It is only when we *imagine the possibility* of their simultaneous coexistence within a single individual's consciousness that we become confused. The realization that the two terms "free will" and "determinism" represent *two different aspects of experience*—each accompanying distinct social roles of the individual—allows us to dispel the paradoxes surrounding them.

Intuitive feelings of will and choice exist in all individuals as they go about their ordinary lives. When one individual is subjected to the scrutiny of another, the latter may conclude that the former's behavior is determined. As a result of such "objective" evidence, it is frequently claimed that the feeling of free will is an illusion, or an epiphenomenon, having no actual involvement in the mechanistic physical world of events. But the observer neglects to turn the analysis back upon his own behavior as observer. To do so would represent a never-ending process that cannot establish a fixed reality of absolute events. The observer does not include his own brain and behavior within the mechanical picture of the world he has created—which would destroy the internal beauty and self-contained logic of the picture.

Einstein recognized the importance of relating a description of the physical world to the motion of the observer within it. Heisenberg's Uncertainty Principle recognizes the influence of the observer as an active force in the described system. Nevertheless, we persist in thinking of a described system as representing an external reality of physical events to which we have limited access, rather than admitting that it also reflects internal body and brain processes of the describer. There have been exceptions to this dominant viewpoint, as expressed, for example, by Eddington, Jeans, Pauli and de Broglie. But these scientists tended to lean to the opposite extreme of monism when they began to describe the world as constituted purely of "mind-stuff." Instead, the kind of world concept I have tried to develop here is that of an *infinitely* complex and therefore unknowable universe in which certain experienced events disclose themselves in consciousness through the evolution of central nervous processes having adaptive value in maintaining bodily homeostasis.

Feelings of will are not usually considered to affect the perceptions of an impartial, analytic observer. Although an observer may have a hypothesis or theory concerning the pattern of events in nature, any measurements taken should not be influenced by the hypothesis. Instead, nature supposedly is left to take its course within the circumscribed limits defined by an experiment, and the outcome of the experiment should, independent of the observer's expectations, confirm or disconfirm the hypothesis. This is an ideal view of science, but does it exist?

There have been few attempts to confirm or disconfirm its existence in such a pure form. However, Rosenthal (1966) has claimed that the outcome of psychological experiments can be unconsciously influenced by the hypothesis of the scientist. When separate identical experiments were conducted on a homogeneous population of subjects by two different observers who were testing opposite predictions, the results obtained in each case favored the particular hypothesis of each respective observer. Unfortunately, Rosenthal's position leads to an infinite circular regression of successive explanations of observations, since if valid it must apply to Rosenthal's investigations themselves. For unless Rosenthal and his colleagues wish to claim themselves as uniquely not subject to their own conclusions (which can hardly be justified), their own results must have been influenced by their own preconceived hypothesis that experimental results are affected by preconceived hypotheses!

Where then does this leave us with regard to the results of experimental psychology? If Rosenthal's hypothesis *is* valid, then a totally objective psychology cannot exist. But in that case it follows that we cannot know whether or not Rosenthal's results are valid! On the other hand if Rosenthal's hypothesis *is not* valid, then we can accept the consensus of findings in experimental psychology and reject Rosenthal's results. But to do so we have to disconfirm Rosenthal's results by experiment—thereby fulfilling the falsifiability requirement of science. In the process of doing so we may unconsciously, in accordance with Rosenthal's hypothesis, influence the results so as to disconfirm Rosenthal's hypothesis! Clearly, there is no escape from this maze of contradictions if we cannot devise "motiveless experiments." This applies not only to behavioral science but to physical science too, where measurements must ultimately be taken at some point by an observer. If this is the case, then consensus between large numbers of independent investigators in obtaining similar results could depend to some extent on the persuasive effects of careful theoretical argument in scientific journals.

The dilemma presented by Rosenthal's hypothesis stems from the assumption that the hypothesis must necessarily relate to some kind of knowable "objective reality." Instead, we must recognize that knowledge cannot exist independently of human acts and consciousness. Therefore, that which we call "knowledge" represents *a system of belief,* which varies from one culture to another and is indispensable to the maintenance of the structural characteristics of each culture. This is the conclusion borne out by the work of Malinowski, Whorf, and, from a different perspective, Lévi-Strauss.

Malinowski (1955) described how magical ceremonies in "primitive cultures," which are considered by us to be wishful, noneffective acts, are not regarded that way by members of the cultures themselves. They believe their acts to be as effective for them in their control of nature as we believe our scientifically based technological acts to be effective for us. A member of an alien culture might consider our donning of white coats and mixing of noxious, odorous fluids in glass vials magical acts, especially whenever a chemical factory explodes contrary to our intentions. We explain the cause of such disasters as "accidents," in which unknown or unforeseen events intrude into the normal orderly scheme of operations. Likewise, if a magical ceremony does not bring about the desired result, a South Seas Islander might explain the failure by saying the ceremony wasn't performed properly or "something went wrong," the same as we do in explaining the failures of our technology. In other words, secondary hypotheses and *ex post facto* explanations are invoked to maintain the basic system of belief.*

If we recognize the fact that the will *necessarily* enters into all scientific observations, then it follows that the correctness or incorrectness of Rosenthal's hypothesis is not directly called into question. Since Rosenthal's hypothesis cannot be falsified, the question is meaningless. All that can be said is that the results that Rosenthal obtained are consistent with his belief in the hypothesis that "experimenters tend to obtain the results they anticipate." It is also once more apparent that this particular example of an attempt to explain the nature of a system from within the system is ultimately impossible. Rosenthal's results are simply another example of the ritual belief in science in Western cultures and can be presumed to represent a functional aspect of that culture. This system of scientific belief does not represent any greater or lesser degree of knowable external reality than any other magical ritual in the same or different culture. Various systems of belief differ in their effectiveness in maintaining the homeostasis of the individual members of the various

---

*In drawing attention to the similarities in the belief systems of magical and scientific cultures I do not wish to imply that the effectiveness of each practice is also similar. The relative efficacy of magic and science constitutes a different problem that I shall not pursue here.

cultures. Systems of belief, therefore, only have validity or invalidity relative to survival (of individuals and societies) and do not differ in the degree to which they approximate a universal "truth."

The purpose of scientific observation is described as extending beyond the immediate behavioral context, as being in the interests of the pursuit of "knowledge." We do not as a rule take into consideration any personal motivations of the scientist that might relate to his social status and the gains that might accrue to him as a result of his investigations. The overall nature of scientific observations is concealed to some extent by the form in which they are reported—the use of the third person and the passive voice—in order to reduce the intrusion of intention and will into the system of knowledge, so that it can be regarded as absolute and independent of the consciousness of the investigator.

Although the experimenter may not exert his will so as to obtain certain expected results, he does exert his will in order to obtain results of some kind or other—he does, after all, will the experiment itself. Even if scientific results are regarded as independent of the will of the observer, they are nevertheless subsequently applied directively in technological acts willed toward the achievement of specific utilitarian goals. The dependence of advanced Western societies on technique has been emphasized by Ellul (1964). Heisenberg (1958) perceived science and technology as a gigantic biological process with utilitarian values.

> The enormous success of this combination of natural and technical science led to a strong preponderance of those nations or states or communities in which this kind of human activity flourished, and as a natural consequence of this activity had to be taken up even by those

nations which by tradition would not have been inclined toward natural and technical sciences. The modern means of communication and of traffic finally completed this process of expansion of technical civilization. Undoubtedly the process has fundamentally changed the conditions of life on our earth and whether one approves of it or not, whether one calls it progress or danger, one must realize that it has gone far beyond any control through human forces. One may rather consider it as a biological process on the largest scale whereby the structures active in the human organism encroach on larger parts of matter and transform it into a state suited for the increasing human population.

Physical science is founded on the premise that natural phenomena can be explained by mechanical laws, independent of any metaphysical forces, which cannot be depicted in terms of space–time representation. In the life sciences this premise is extended to the physiology and behavior of organisms. A sequence of physically determined events is sought in the form of transformations of motion from physical elements external to the body to those within the body. Concepts such as "will" and "consciousness," which cannot be represented in space–time coordinates, do not enter into a physical description of bodily events.

Let us examine the phenomenological distinctions between physical and metaphysical forces, taking gravity as an example of a physical force. Gravity is not perceived directly in the same way that color can be said to be perceived directly. It is inferred either from the perceived motions of objects or from the need to postulate a hypothetical counteractive force whenever a body is motionless but known to be subject to the influence of an established force, for example, the tension of a spring in the case of a weight hanging from a balance. Forces acting without the visible movement of physical matter are conceived in terms of the kinesthetic sense of exertion experienced whenever the muscles are tensed without gross movement of the body (isometric contraction).

Gravity is inferred from its *effects* on bodies, in the form of movement or stress. The concepts of movement and stress are derived, circularly, from the experience of the imputed effects of gravity on our own living bodies. When standing upright we feel pressure on our feet and tension in our "antigravity" muscles, which are contracted so as to hold the skeleton in equilibrium. When falling freely through the air, deformations of the body occur as we accelerate from rest because of inequalities in acceleration of the various body parts; these deformations are accompanied by unique conscious experiences associated with somatosensory afferent activity. When a uniform velocity in free fall has been attained, this somatosensory activity disappears (assuming a vacuum and, therefore, absence of wind) and the only afferent "effects" of gravity are visual, i.e., the motion of the eyes relative to the environment. Analogously, the single effect of the sun's gravity we experience on the earth is that of visual motion of the cosmos.

Thus, although physical forces are not perceived directly, their *effects* are perceived, and quantitative measurements of those effects are taken that yield mathematical relations in the form of laws. These quantified relations are the characteristics by which physical forces are distinguished from metaphysical forces. When motions of bodies occur that do not obey known physical laws, it is assumed that other physical (as yet unobserved) forces must exist as causes. But it is also assumed that the unknown forces should manifest themselves through some kind of measurable orderly effect visually perceivable as motion.

In nuclear physics the existence of the subatomic particles—such as electrons, positrons, protons, and neutrons—is inferred from visual "tracks" left in bubble chambers. The existence of neutrinos is inferred from recoil-like deflections in the tracks of positrons whenever the latter decay. Tracks of neutrinos themselves have never been observed, and when originally proposed neutrinos were considered to be imaginary particles. The visual effects of quarks, which are presumed to be the constituents of protons, neutrons, and electrons, have yet to be actually observed as deflections in the tracks of other particles. Unlike physical forces, metaphysical forces are not inferred in a quantitative manner. Although metaphysical forces may be invoked in explanations of unusual physical events, they are not regarded as having explanatory power because they do not help to introduce any formal order into the perceived motions such that they no longer appear unusual.

The attempt to reduce the various kinds of physical forces—heat, light, electricity, magnetism, and gravitation—to a single energy represents a further step in our imagination. But it is at this point that the Western scientific view meets with the mystical views of nature in other cultures. Energy is conceived as a force that manifests itself in a variety of different forms, but with all of them having the common characteristic of wave formation. These waves of energy capable of flowing through a vacuum are not so very different from those invisible metaphysical forces of *prakriti* in Indian Vedic philosophy or of *Tao* in Taoism, which are considered to be a manifestation of an all-encompassing God. The Judeo-Christian God is considered to be a Prime Mover who created the universe and set it moving, by breathing into it the various forces responsible for the observed motions. Although most scientists today do not identify energy with a god, energy is considered to be invisible, only manifesting itself indirectly by way of its effects in producing motions of physical bodies. Inevitably, a god appears where our direct perceptions end.

The concept of force stems from the experiences of will and exertion that accompany bodily movements that result in movement of external physical objects, or the experience of motion of our own bodies relative to a substrate. Energy thus represents a projection of our experience of will and force out into the universe. Whereas Schopenhauer (1883) considered the experience of will in human consciousness to be one particular expression of a larger Will inherent within the whole of nature, the foregoing analysis leads me to think of the experience of the will as an aspect of evolution confined to "higher" animals, one that helps to guide action and promote survival.

Modern physics was made possible by the mathematical conception of Cartesian coordinates. The motions of energy sources are portrayed in pure mathematics in coordinates measured along three orthogonal axes from their point of intersection. When we actually measure physical phenomena, however, no such abstract, stable origin exists independent of the observer—all measurements in reality must be relative to the observer. But once the observer enters the picture, an independent, absolute external reality can no longer exist. Einstein recognized the importance of the position and motion of the observer's sense organs relative to the perceived external phenomena, but he did not go further and consider the involvement of the observer's brain processes and consciousness, or the effects of evolution of the brain, in the determination of physical phenomena. Clearly, the observer cannot measure his own behavior in measuring external physical phenomena; a second observer is needed to do this; and a third observer to measure that of the second; and so on. A self-contained picture of the universe can never be completed.

It is only through consciousness that any kind of intellectual picture of the world can emerge in the first place. As Nietzsche, Spengler, and Bergson all realized, there really is no problem concerning free will and determinism, since determinism is a product of the intellect and therefore of the will. The utility of determinism as an idea is its ability to *predict the effects of our actions on the world.* Although the system of physical science represents the effects of our actions on the inanimate world, the living body and its behavior and consciousness are taken for granted and not analyzed within the system. In this sense, consciousness is coextensive with the system. When we proceed to study life itself as a physical process, we continue to covertly involve the living body and its behavior in the analysis.

Even though the effects of our actions on the world can be predicted, the actions themselves cannot. Wittgenstein (1955) pointed out the relationship between the indeterminancy of future actions and "knowledge" of their effects.

> All inference takes place *a priori.*
> From an elementary proposition no other can be inferred.

In no way can an inference be made from the existence of one state of affairs to the existence of another entirely different from it.

There is no causal nexus which justifies such an inference.

The events of the future *cannot* be inferred from those of the present.

Superstition is the belief in the causal nexus.

The freedom of the will consists in the fact that future actions cannot be known now. We could only know them if causality were an inner necessity, like that of logical deduction. — The connexion of knowledge and what is known is that of a logical necessity.

Ontogenetically, the experience of the will precedes the experience of determinism. The world of the child is dominated by the experience of the will. Piaget (1952) conceives the child's actions in terms of their accommodation to the "intrinsic nature" of the external world, and of the assimilation of certain features of the world into the "intrinsic nature" of the child. Only in the later stages of intellectual development are events in the world perceived as occurring independent of a personal ego and will. Ontogenetically, assimilation is prior to accommodation and will is prior to causality and knowledge.

8 Psyclosis

I am nearing closure of the circle of thought traced in this book. I began by describing how motions of the body evolved from cyclic alterations in geophysical events, and how from these motions a sense of time arose, which was subsequently reified in those selfsame geophysical events. Once a sense of time arises, self-consciousness can be said to occur. Self-perception, of one's own existence and motion, is thus dependent on an external world of events. But once self-con-sciousness is attained, it will eventually discover its own origin by completion of a circle of conceptions. Complete self-consciousness is reached when its evolu-tionary history is fully understood. At that point an ob-jective reality no longer exists, and thought will have circled back to its origin.

Spengler has beautifully described how this circularity is expressed in the birth, growth, and death of individual cultures. From the debris of each dead culture new forms of consciousness arise that inevitably trace out a new belief system, which may be expressed in a new civilization.

A sense of time creates a past and future, as reflected in memory and expectancy, respectively. Expectancy of the future is associated with will and choice. Instinctual reflexes might "anticipate" future effects, but they cannot consciously project themselves into a future. However, whenever a fixed reflex or acquired habit fails to achieve the ends initially responsible for its development, consciousness turns towards the events surrounding the act. In an animal capable of predictive learning, will springs to the fore and alternative acts are imagined as potential ways of achieving the same ends as the original reflex. The future comes about because of the will, either through habits (acquired by past expressions of the will) or through conscious choice (present expressions of the will).

To ask the question whether the future can exist without consciousness is therefore to ask a meaningless question. Without memory the past does not exist, and without a past the future cannot be anticipated. The past does not exist in physical form (not even in the form of tree rings) but only in symbolic form. A universe without memory would only constitute a succession of instant experiences, each complete within itself. Time is a biological *a priori* intuition. Whorf (1956) described how the subjective nature of time is expressed in different ways in the languages of separate cultures.

> When we speak of "ten steps forward," "ten strokes on a bell," or any similarly described cyclic sequence, "times" of any sort, we are doing the same thing as with "days."

CYCLICITY brings the response of imaginary plurals. But a likeness of cyclicity to aggregates is not unmistakably given by experience prior to language, or it would be found in all languages and it is not.

Our AWARENESS of time and cyclicity does contain something immediate and subjective—the basic sense of "becoming later and later.".... This ... should not be called subjective. I call it OBJECTIFIED or imaginary, because it is patterned on the OUTER world.... A "length of time" is envisioned as a row of similar units, like a row of bottles.

Our "length of time" is not regarded [in Hopi] as a length but as a relation between two events in lateness. Instead of our linguistically promoted objectification of that datum of consciousness we call "time," the Hopi language has not laid down any pattern that would cloak the subjective "becoming later" that is the essence of (Hopi) time.

Here Whorf brings out how the subjective "becoming later," which is the essence of time, is "objectified" and therefore imaginary. The whole system of Western scientific thought is inextricably linked with time as an externalized concept. Therefore, following Whorf's thesis, the system is "objectified and imaginary." The fact that it consistently relates so many aspects of phenomenal experience with one another does not necessarily imply that it is a veridical description of external events in themselves, but instead should be taken to indicate that it reflects a system of operations (in the form of nervous processes and bodily movements) that maintains homeostasis and consistency in our experience of an inferred external world of events. This particular system of knowledge depends on our biological and cultural inheritance as much as it does upon an independent external world of physical events.

I have already stressed how the conception of time in

Western thought is expressed in spatial (and therefore visual) terms. We feel we have grasped the essence of the internal feeling of becoming when we have objectified it by measuring it in spatial terms. Whenever we perform measurements we ultimately rely on sight—a direct result of the exquisite sensitivity and resolution of our visual systems. Even when we measure the weight of an object with a balance we use vision instead of our somatosensory systems. We do not weigh masses by comparing the feelings of heaviness of an object held in one hand with that of an arbitrary standard held in the other. Instead we devise a mechanical balance and rely upon a visual measure of spatial position in order to measure weight. If we had to depend solely upon somatosensory information in weighing things we would be limited to weighing only those objects that we could pick up manually or with a machine. But we transcend this mechanical limitation by use of visual geometry. Once we have measured the density of an object by using a balance, we can "weigh" an object of the same density by measuring its visual dimensions and other factors. By this method we "weigh" the earth, sun, and moon. We weigh them by way of the visual system. Time itself is also measured visually, as in the movement of the sun's shadow, the hands of a watch, or of an electric current.

If we conceived time in the same way as the Hopi Indians—as a "becoming later" rather than as a spatial length—time would be identified with life itself rather than as a physical entity external to life. Our view of time as external is exemplified in our analysis of life, which is characterized by cyclic motions within the organism and of the organism as a whole. This view is not derived from our internal experience; instead, we feel a continual "becoming." If this were not the case we could not have an awareness of evolution and change. Everything would appear to be a repetition of that which had occurred before—a world of physical materialism where everything changed in an inexorable, recurrent, predetermined manner. One premise of "objective" physical science is that the sense of change and evolution is an illusion and merely represents the compound effect of a relatively small number of eternal universal laws concerning the properties of matter, including the matter that composes living bodies. I have argued for a contrary view—that physical determinism is an illusion when considered from within itself.

The realization that the experience of time cannot be reduced to a more fundamental experience—that it is an elemental aspect of our human consciousness—also leads to the realization that all knowable events in nature are based upon cyclic images. Our image of the universe is that of a gigantic wound-up clock inexorably moving in a cyclic fashion. Since formal analysis is a biological product, it must also display cyclic characteristics. The starting point of any formal analysis (including this present one) is arbitrary. Whether one begins with "external reality" or with "the body" or with "experience" is unimportant, since the analysis must circulate through each of these concepts and eventually return to whichever one was chosen at the beginning. Formal analysis therefore constitutes a tautology. Wittgenstein (1955) clearly saw this.

> *The limits of my language* mean the limits of my world.
> Logic fills the world, the limits of the world are also its limits. . . .
> The fact that the propositions of logic are tautologies shows the formal—logical—properties of language of the world.

That its constituent parts connected together *in this* way give a tautology characterizes the logic of its constituent parts.

In order that propositions connected together in a definite way may give a tautology they must have definite properties of structure. That they give a tautology when *so* connected shows therefore that they possess these properties of structure. . . .

Logic is not a theory but a reflection of the world.

Logic is transcendental.

Mathematics is a logical method.

The propositions of mathematics are equations, and therefore pseudo-propositions.

Mathematical propositions express no thoughts.

The logic of the world which the propositions of logic show in tautologies, mathematics shows in equations. . . .

A necessity for one thing to happen because another has happened does not exist. There is only *logical* necessity.

At the basis of the whole modern view of the world lies the illusion that the so-called laws of nature are the explanations of natural phenomena. . . .

We feel that even if *all possible* scientific questions be answered, the problems of life still have not been touched at all. Of course there is then no question left, and just this is the answer.

The solution of the problem of life is seen in the vanishing of this problem.

There is indeed the inexpressible. This shows itself; it is the mystical. . . .

The cycle is the unifying characteristic of both animate and inanimate nature—it casts its image over everything. A seemingly endless list of cyclic events can be drawn up: curvature of space, rotation of the planets, movement of tides and waves, recurrence of the seasons, bodily synthesis of biochemicals, firing of the nerve cell, circulation of the blood, sleep and wakefulness, birth, growth, and death of the body, fashions of hair length and clothes, population and economic cycles, etc. Only the process of evolution itself appears to be nonrecurrent.

But we must recognize the temporal limits to our knowledge of the history of the universe. Events seen on the largest possible scale may appear linear but need not actually be so. Certainly the possibility is open of reversal of the Second Law of Thermodynamics when applied to the universe as a whole, and is seriously considered by those who believe in a recurrent expansion and contraction of the universe (e.g., Gold, 1962). Our window onto universal events is restricted. Events that appear to be linear from our own standpoint in time might appear as a fragment of a cyclic pattern of events were they to be viewed from a broader perspective, as depicted in Figure 17. Just as in the past the earth was considered to be flat, so may our conception of the linear progression of the evolution of the universe be the result of our limited perspective.

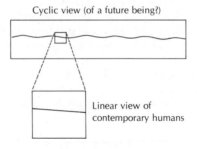

Cyclic view (of a future being?)

Linear view of contemporary humans

FIGURE 17

If everything in nature is recurrent or circular, then so must intellectual thought. Certainly, belief systems of entire cultures exhibit cycles of birth, growth, and death, as described by Spengler. But circulation of thought also applies to individual theories. As Eddington (1928) showed to be the case for Einstein's theory of general relativity, all theories are tautologies, whether they are physical, like Einstein's; biological, like Darwin's; behavioral, like Skinner's; psychological, like Freud's; philosophical, like Nietzsche's; or historical, like Spengler's. I have already discussed the circularity of Darwin's and Skinner's theories; by way of further illustration let us briefly consider the circularity of Freudian theory and Nietzsche's philosophic system.

In Freudian theory intellectual thought is considered to be dependent upon underlying unconscious processes involving instinctual emotions and early childhood experiences. But if Freudian theory is valid, it must necessarily apply to the thought processes involved in its own genesis—within Freud himself. In order to carry the theory to its logical conclusion, it would be necessary to analyze the personal events of Freud's individual life in order to understand the derivation of his own theory. But by doing so the theory becomes circular. The completion of this circular thought process would throw into relief the theory's personal nature, whereas the theory was originally postulated by Freud to be universal in its application. Freudian theory is thereby reduced to a personal view of the universe and one usually considered closer to art than to science.

Nietzsche (1968) disclosed the relativity of consciousness and its values to the preservation of the body.

> In the tremendous multiplicity of events within an organism, the part which becomes conscious to us is a mere means: and the little bit of "virtue," "selflessness," and similar functions are refuted radically by the total bal-

ance of events. We should study our organism in all its immorality—

The animal functions are, as a matter of principle, a million times more important than all our beautiful moods and heights of consciousness: the latter are a surplus, except when they have to serve as tools of those animal functions. The entire *conscious* life, the spirit along with the soul, the heart, goodness, and virtue—in whose service do they labor? In the service of the greatest possible perfection of the means (means of nourishment, means of enhancement) of the basic animal functions: above all, the enhancement of life.

What one used to call "body" and "flesh" is of such unspeakably greater importance: the remainder is a small accessory. The task of spinning on the chain of life, and in such a way that the thread grows ever more powerful— that is the task.

But consider how heart, soul, virtue, spirit practically conspire together to subvert this systematic task—as if *they* were the end in view! — The degeneration of life is conditioned essentially by the extraordinary proneness to error of consciousness: it is held in check by instinct the least of all and therefore blunders the longest and the most thoroughly.

To measure whether existence has value according to the pleasant and unpleasant feelings aroused in this consciousness: can one think of a madder extravagance of vanity? For it is only a means—and pleasant or unpleasant feelings are also only means!

What is the objective measure of value? Solely the quantum of enhanced and organized power.

But these same considerations must also apply to Neitzche's own consciousness and philosophical ideas, which thereby devalues any internal validity they may possess independent of a subsequent *a posteriori* analysis of their biological adaptive value in preserving the body. Nietzsche acknowledged this fact himself.

> That the value of the world lies in our interpretation (—that other interpretations than merely human ones are perhaps somewhere possible—); that previous interpretations have been perspective valuations by virtue of which we can survive in life, i.e., in the will to power, for the growth of power; that every elevation of man brings with it the overcoming of narrower interpretations; that every strengthening and increase of power opens up new perspectives and means believing in new horizons—this idea permeates my writings. The world with which we are concerned is false, i.e., is not a fact but a fable and approximation on the basis of a meager sum of observations; it is "in flux," as something in a state of becoming, as a falsehood always changing but never getting near the truth: for—there is no "truth."

Circularity also applies to the work presented here. It too has returned to its origin and revealed its tautologous nature. If all thought must ultimately circulate back upon itself, then all epistemologies are historically relative to their points in time and cultural "location," and are composed of an endless progression of circular theories that are interrelated and interdependent. If consciousness and knowledge exist relative to their functions in sustaining the body, then cognition is also biologically, culturally, and historically relative.

This thesis constitutes a humanistic outlook that argues against reifying our experiences in an absolute realm of independent events external to our bodies. Instead we should respect the relativity of this experience to the kingdom of the body, which it serves. Clearly this statement could be negated by a subsequent one pointing out the first statement's relativity to this moment in Western cultural and intellectual history. But then a third statement could be leveled in a similar vein at the second, and so on . . . One must stop at some point, if only to argue against the futility of an excursion to reach an epistemological terminus—there can be no such terminus.

I conclude this work with the realization that its viewpoint is no more than one manifestation of the overall circulation of Western intellectual thought towards its origin. This viewpoint has no universal significance, since, as I hope I have shown, such would be inconsistent with the view itself. We have come to recognize the protean quality and limitations of cognition and its dependence on the body. The history of Western thought is that of a mind that first considered the world to be an external reality independent of the body; later it discovered its own traces in the external world; next it turned to an examination of those traces and their origin in the body; finally it scrutinizes itself and external reality slips away as a fleeting image that has served its purpose.

Apocalyptic visions of the future, such as that of Norman O. Brown (1973), are symptomatic of the times themselves and do not represent any absolute reality. They will in due course pass away with our culture to give way to the birth of a new vision—one that is, initially, more optimistic. As Nietzsche showed us, the ascent and exhilaration of the mountain top must inevitably be followed by the descent to the valley. Humans cannot live permanently on an intellectual crest, but must ascend and descend just as animals are forced to repeatedly migrate back and forth across the globe. Different intellectual vistas will arise as life unfolds, each of which will be unique and valid within and unto itself—little more can be said than this.

I conclude, as I began, with a quotation from Baudelaire. "In philosophical studies, the human mind mirrors the revolution of the spheres, and is obliged to follow a curve that will return it to the point of its departure. To conclude is only to complete a circle."

References

Annis, R. C., and B. Frost. 1973. Human visual ecology and orientation anisotropies in acuity. *Science,* **182:** 729–731.

Asch, S. E., and H. A. Witkin. 1948. Studies in space orientation. II. Perception of the upright with displaced visual fields and with body tilted. *Journal of Experimental Psychology,* **38:** 455–477.

Aserinsky, E., and N. Kleitman. 1953. Regularly occurring periods of eye motility, and concomitant phenomena, during sleep. *Science,* **118:** 273–274.

Ball, G. G. 1974. Vagotomy: Effect on electrically elicited eating and self-stimulation in the lateral hypothalamus. *Science,* **184:** 484–485.

Barlow, H. B., C. Blakemore, and J. D. Pettigrew. 1967. The neural mechanism of binocular depth discrimination. *Journal of Physiology (London),* **193:** 327–342.

Batteau, D. W. 1968. Listening with the naked ear. In *The Neuropsychology of Spatially Oriented Behavior,* S. J. Freedman, ed. Homewood, Illinois: Dorsey Press, pp. 109–133.

Békésy, G. von. 1967. *Sensory Inhibition.* Princeton University Press.

Bélanger, D., and S. M. Feldman, 1962. Effects of water deprivation on heart rate and instrumental activity in the rat. *Journal of Comparative and Physiological Psychology,* **55:** 220–225.

Benedict, R. 1959. *Patterns of Culture,* 2nd ed. Boston: Houghton-Mifflin.

Berger, R. J. 1963. Experimental modification of dream content by meaningful verbal stimuli. *British Journal of Psychiatry,* **109:** 722–740.

———. 1967. When is a dream is a dream is a dream? *Experimental Neurology,* Supplement No. 4: 15–28.

———. 1969a. Physiological characteristics of sleep. In *Sleep: Physiology and Pathology,* A. Kales, ed. Philadelphia: Lippincott, pp. 66–79.

Berger, R. J. 1969b. The sleep and dream cycle. *Ibid*, pp. 17–32.

———. 1975. Bioenergetic functions of sleep and activity rhythms and their possible relevance to aging. *Federation Proceedings*, **34**: 97–102.

Bergson, H. L., 1910. *Time and Free Will*. New York: Macmillan.

———. 1937. *Creative Evolution*, translated by A. Mitchell. New York: Holt.

Berman, A. J., and D. Berman. 1973. Fetal deafferentation: The ontogenesis of movement in the absence of peripheral sensory feedback. *Experimental Neurology*, **38**: 170–176.

Bertalanffy, L. von. 1969. *General System Theory: Foundations, Development, Applications*. New York: Braziller.

Blakemore, C. 1974. Developmental factors in the formation of feature extracting neurons. In *The Neurosciences, Third Study Program*, F. O. Schmitt and F. G. Worden, eds. Cambridge, Mass.: MIT Press, pp. 105–113.

Blakemore, C., and G. F. Cooper. 1970. Development of the brain depends on the visual environment. *Nature*, **228**: 477–478.

Blakemore, C., and D. E. Mitchell. 1973. Environmental modification of the visual cortex and the neural basis of learning and memory. *Nature*, **241**: 467–468.

Bligh, J. 1973. *Temperature Regulation in Mammals and Other Vertebrates*. New York: Elsevier.

Bornstein, M. H. 1973. Color vision and color naming: A psychophysiological hypothesis of cultural difference. *Psychological Bulletin*, **80**: 257–285.

Brown, N. O. 1973. *Closing Time*. New York: Random House.

Cannon, W. R. 1932. *The Wisdom of the Body*. New York: Norton.

Carew, T. J., V. F. Castellucci, E. R. Kandel. 1971. An analysis of dishabituation and sensitization of the gill-withdrawal reflex in *Aplysia*. *International Journal of Neuroscience*, **2**: 79–98.

Chomsky, N. 1968. *Language and Mind*. New York: Harcourt, Brace, Jovanovich.

Corning, W. C., and S. Kelley. 1973. Platyhelminthes: The turbellarians. In *Invertebrate Learning, Volume I, Protozoans through Annelids,* W. C. Corning, J. A. Dyal, and A. O. D. Willows, eds. New York: Plenum Press, pp. 171–224.

Davies, P. C. W. 1974. *The Physics of Time Asymmetry.* London: Surrey University Press.

Davis, W. J. 1973. Development of locomotor patterns in absence of peripheral sense organs and muscles. *Proceedings of the National Academy of Sciences U.S.A.,* **70**: 954–958.

De Valois, R. L., and G. H. Jacobs. 1968. Primate color vision. *Science,* **162**: 533–540.

Dement, W., and N. Kleitman. 1957. Cyclic variations in EEG during sleep and their relation to eye movements, body motility, and dreaming. *Electroencephalography and Clinical Neurophysiology,* **9**: 673–690.

Dement, W. C. and E. A. Wolpert. 1958. The relation of eye movements, body motility, and external stimuli to dream content. *Journal of Experimental Psychology,* **55**: 543–553.

Ditchburn, R. W., and B. L. Ginsborg. 1952. Vision with a stabilized retinal image. *Nature,* **170**: 36–37.

Eccles, J. C. 1970. *Facing Reality.* New York: Springer Verlag.

Eddington, A. S. 1928. *The Nature of the Physical World.* New York: Macmillan.

Eisman, E. 1966. Effects of deprivation and consummatory activity on heart rate. *Journal of Comparative and Physiological Psychology,* **62**: 71–75.

Ellul, J. 1964. *The Technological Society,* translated by John Wilkinson. New York: Knopf.

Festinger, L., C. A. Burnham, H. Ono, and D. Bamber. 1967. Efference and the conscious experience of perception. *Journal of Experimental Psychology Monograph,* **74**(4): 1–36.

Festinger, L. and L. K. Cannon. 1965. Information about spatial location based on knowledge about efference. *Psychological Review,* **72**: 373–384.

Foulkes, D. 1966. *The Psychology of Sleep*. New York: Scribner.

Freud, S. 1953. The Interpretation of Dreams. In *The Standard Edition of the Complete Psychological Works*, Vols. 4 and 5. London: Hogarth Press.

———. 1964. New Introductory Lectures on Psychoanalysis. *Ibid*, Vol. 22.

Garcia, J., and R. A. Koelling. 1966. Relation of cue to consequence in avoidance learning. *Psychonomic Science*, **4**: 123–124.

Garstang, W. 1928. The morphology of the tunicata and its bearings on the phylogeny of the chordata. *Quarterly Journal of Microscopical Science*, **72**: 51.

Gelb, A. 1929. Die "Farbenkonstanz" der Sehdinge. *Handbuch der normalen und pathologischen Physiologie*, **12**(1): 594–678.

Georgescu-Roegen, N. 1971. *The Entropy Law and the Economic Process*. Harvard University Press.

Gibson, J. J. 1933. Adaptation after-effect and contrast in the perception of curved lines. *Journal of Experimental Psychology*, **16**: 1–31.

———. 1966. *The Senses Considered as Perceptual Systems*. Boston: Houghton Mifflin.

Gold, T. 1962. Arrow of time. In *Recent Developments in General Relativity*, New York: Pergammon-Macmillan.

Goldstein, K. *The Organism*. New York: American Book.

Goodenough, D. R., J. Sapan, J. Cohen, G. Portnoff, and A. Shapiro. 1971. Some experiments concerning the effects of sleep on memory. *Psychophysiology*, **8**: 749–762.

Goodwin, D. W., B. Powell, D. Bremer, H. Hoine, and J. Stern. 1969. Alcohol and recall: State-dependent effects in man. *Science*, **163**: 1358–1360.

Gregory, R. L., and J. G. Wallace. 1963. Recovery from early blindness. *Experimental Psychology Society Monographs*, No. 2.

Groves, P. M., and R. F. Thompson. 1970. Habituation: A dual-process theory. *Psychological Review*, **77**: 419–450.

Grüsser-Cornehls, U., O. Grüsser, and T. H. Bullock. 1963. Unit responses in the frog's tectum to moving and non-moving visual stimuli. *Science*, **141**: 820–822.

Hall, C. S., and V. J. Nordby. 1972. *The Individual and his Dreams*. New York: New American Library.

———. 1973. *A Primer of Jungian Psychology*. New York: New American Library.

Hamburger, V. 1970. Embryonic motility in vertebrates. *The Neurosciences, Second Study Program*, F. O. Schmitt, ed. New York: Rockefeller University Press, pp. 141–151.

Hebb, D. O. 1949. *The Organization of Behavior*. New York: Wiley.

Heisenberg, W. 1958. *Physics and Philosophy*. New York: Harper.

Held, R. 1965. Plasticity in sensory-motor systems. *Scientific American*, **213**(5): 84–94.

Held, R., and J. A. Bauer, Jr. 1967. Visually guided reaching in infant monkeys after restricted rearing. *Science*, **155**: 718–720.

Held, R., and A. Hein. 1963. Movement produced stimulation in the development of visually guided behavior. *Journal of Comparative and Physiological Psychology*, **56**: 872–876.

Hill, S. Y., R. Schwin, B. Powell, and D. W. Goodwin. 1973. State-dependent effects of Marihuana on human memory. *Nature*, **243**: 241–242.

Hirsch, H. V. B., and D. N. Spinelli. 1971. Modification of the distribution of receptive field orientation in cats by selective visual exposure during development. *Experimental Brain Research*, **13**: 509–527.

Hoagland, H. 1933. The physiological control of judgements of duration: Evidence for a chemical clock. *Journal of General Psychology*, **9**: 267–287.

Hubel, D. H., and T. N. Wiesel. 1959. Receptive fields of single neurones in the cat's striate cortex. *Journal of Physiology (London)*, **148**: 574–591.

———. 1962. Receptive fields, binocular interaction, and

functional architecture in the cat's visual cortex. *Journal of Physiology (London)*, **160**: 106–154.

————. 1963. Receptive fields of cells in striate cortex of very young, visually inexperienced kittens. *Journal of Neurophysiology*, **26**: 994–1002.

Hume, D. A. 1888. *A Treatise of Human Nature*. L. A. Selby-Bigge (Ed.) Oxford: Clarendon Press, p. 93.

Husserl, E. 1964. *The Phenomenology of Internal Time Consciousness*. Indiana University Press.

Jennings, H. S. 1923. *The Behavior of Lower Organisms*. New York: Columbia University Press.

Jung, C. G. 1953. Two essays on analytical psychology. In *The Collected Works of C. G. Jung*, Vol. 7. London: Routledge and Kegan Paul, p. 238.

————. 1960a. The structure and dynamics of the psyche. In *Collected Works*, Vol. 8. Princeton University Press, p. 53.

————. 1960b. On the Nature of Dreams. In *The Collected Works of C. G. Jung*, Vol. 8, London: Routledge and Kegan Paul, pp. 281–297.

————. 1960c. Synchronicity: An acausal connecting principle. In *ibid.*, pp. 417–531.

Kawai, M. 1965. Newly acquired pre-cultural behavior of the natural troop of Japanese monkeys on Koshima islet. *Primates*, **6**: 1–30.

Konishi, M. 1965. The role of auditory feedback in the control of vocalization in the white-crowned sparrow. *Zeitschrift für Tierpsychologie*, **22**: 770–783.

Konorski, J. 1967. *Integrative Activity of the Brain*. University of Chicago Press.

Koukkou, M., and D. Lehmann. 1968. EEG and memory storage in sleep experiments with humans. *Electroencephalography and Clinical Neurophysiology*, **25**: 455–462.

Kovach, J. K., and E. Hess. 1963. Imprinting: Effects of painful stimulation upon the following response. *Journal of Comparative and Physiological Psychology*, **56**: 461–464.

La Barre, W. 1954. *The Human Animal*. University of Chicago Press.

Laing, R. D. 1967. *The Politics of Experience*, London: Penguin.

Larimer, J. L., and J. R. Tindel. 1966. Sensory modifications of heart rate in crayfish. *Animal Behavior*, **14**: 239–245.

Levine, S., L. Goldman, and G. D. Coover. 1972. Expectancy and the pituitary-adrenal system. In "Physiology, Emotion, and Psychosomatic Illness," *CIBA Foundation Symposium* 8 (new series), Amsterdam: ASP (Elsevier, Excerpta Medica, North-Holland), pp. 281–296.

Lévi-Strauss, C. 1966. *The Savage Mind*. London: Weidenfeld and Nicolson.

Lindsley, D. B. 1951, Emotion. In *Handbook of Experimental Psychology*, S. S. Stevens, ed. New York: Wiley, pp. 473–516.

Lotka, A. J. 1945. The Law of Evolution as a maximal principle. *Human Biology*, **17**: 167–194.

Mach, E. 1942. *Popular Scientific Lectures.* Open Court, pp. 186–235.

Macnamara, J. 1972. Cognitive basis of language learning in infants. *Psychological Review*, **79**: 1–13.

Malinowski, B. 1955. Magic, science, and religion. In *Science, Religion, and Reality*, J. Needham, ed. New York: George Braziller, pp. 23–88.

Marler, P., and M. Tamura. 1964. Culturally transmitted patterns of vocal behavior in sparrows. *Science*, **146**: 1483–1486.

Maslow, A. H. 1954. *Motivation and Personality.* New York: Harper.

Masters, W. J., and J. E. Johnson. 1966. *Human Sexual Response*, Boston: Little, Brown.

Maturana, H. R. 1970. *Biology of Cognition.* Biological Computer Laboratory, University of Illinois, Urbana-Champaign, Report No. 9.0.

Maxwell, J. C. 1952. *Matter and Motion.* New York: Dover.

Mountcastle, V. B. 1967. The problem of sensing and the neural coding of sensory events. In *The Neurosciences, A Study Program*, G. C. Quarton, T. Melnechuk, F. O. Schmitt, eds. New York: Rockefeller University Press, pp. 393–408.

Muezinger, K. F. 1934. Motivation in learning, I: Electric shock for correct response in the visual discrimination habit. *Journal of Comparative Psychology,* **17**: 267–277.

Munévar, G. 1975. *Radical Knowledge.* Ph.D. thesis, University of California, Berkeley.

Nietzsche, F. 1968. *The Will to Power,* translated by W. Kaufman and R. J. Hollingdale; W. Kaufman, ed. New York: Random House.

———. 1969. *The Wanderer and His Shadow* (1880). Reprinted in *The Genealogy of Morals,* translated by W. Kaufman and R. J. Hollingdale. New York: Vintage, p. 180.

Osgood, C. E. 1952. The nature and measurement of meaning. *Psychological Bulletin,* **49**: 197–237.

Oswald, I., A. M. Taylor, and M. Triesman. 1960. Discriminative responses to stimulation during human sleep. *Brain,* **83**: 440–453.

Overton, D. A. 1964. State-dependent or "dissociated" learning produced with pentobarbitol. *Journal of Comparative and Physiological Psychology,* **57**: 3–12.

Parker, G. H. 1917. The sources of nervous activity. *Science,* **45**: 619–626.

Pavlov, I. P. 1927. *Conditioned Reflexes.* Oxford University Press.

Pearson, K. 1951. *The Grammar of Science.* London: Dent and Sons.

Penfield, W., and T. Rasmussen. 1950. *The Cerebral Cortex of Man.* New York: Macmillan.

Pettigrew, J. D. 1974. The effect of visual experience on the development of stimulus specificity by kitten cortical neurones. *Journal of Physiology (London),* **237**: 49–74.

Piaget, J. 1952. *The Origins of Intelligence in Children.* New York: International Universities Press.

———. 1966. Time perception in children. In *The Voices of Time,* J. T. Fraser, ed. New York: George Braziller, pp. 202–216.

Portnoff, G., F. Baekeland, D. R. Goodenough, I. Karacan, and A. Shapiro. 1966. Retention of verbal materials perceived immediately prior to onset of non-REM sleep. *Perceptual and Motor Skills*, **22**: 751–758.

Price, H. H. 1953. Survival and the idea of another world. *Proceedings of the Society for Psychical Research*, **50**: 1–25.

Prigogine, I. 1967. *Introduction to Thermodynamics of Irreversible Processes*. New York: Interscience.

Puerto, A., J. A. Deutsch, F. Molina, and P. L. Roll. 1976. Rapid discrimination of rewarding nutrient by the upper gastrointestinal tract. *Science*, **192**: 485–487.

Riesen, A. H. 1967. Sensory deprivation. In *Progress in Physiological Psychology*, E. Stellar and J. Sprague, eds. New York: Academic Press, pp. 117–147.

Riggs, L. A., F. Ratcliffe, J. E. Cornsweet, and T. N. Cornsweet, 1953. The disappearance of steadily fixated test-objects. *Journal of the Optical Society of America*, **43**: 495–501.

Rosenthal, R. A. 1966. *Experimenter Effects in Behavioral Research*. New York: Appleton-Century-Crofts.

Schopenhauer, A. 1883. *The World as Will and Idea*. London: Routledge and Kegan Paul.

Seligman, M. E. P. 1970. On the generality of the laws of learning. *Psychological Review*, **77**: 406–418.

Sheer, D. E. 1961. Emotional facilitation in learning situations with subcortical stimulation. In *Electrical Stimulation of the Brain*, D. E. Sheer, ed. Austin: University of Texas Press, pp. 431–464.

Skinner, B. F. 1969. *Contingencies of Reinforcement: A Theoretical Analysis*. New York: Appleton-Century-Crofts.

Smythies, J. R. 1965. The representative theory of perception. In *Brain and Mind*, J. R. Smythies, ed. London: Routledge and Kegan Paul, pp. 241–264.

Sokolov, E. N. 1963. *Perception and the Conditioned Reflex*, translated by S. W. Waydenfeld. New York: Macmillan.

Spengler, O. 1926. *The Decline of the West,* two volumes, translated by C. F. Atkinson. New York: Knopf.

Sperry, R. W. 1969. A modified concept of consciousness. *Psychological Review,* **76**: 532–536.

Stellar, E. 1954. The physiology of motivation. *Psychological Review,* **61**: 5–22.

Stent, G. 1975. Limits to the scientific understanding of man. *Science,* **187**: 1052–1058.

Stevens, S. S. 1957. On the psychophysical law. *Psychological Review,* **64**: 153-181.

Stratton, G. M. 1897. Vision without inversion of the retinal image. *Psychological Review,* **4**: 341–360, 463-481.

Szasz, R. S. 1961. *The Myth of Mental Illness: Foundations of a Theory of Personal Conduct.* New York: Hoeber-Harper.

Tart, C. T. 1972. States of consciousness and state-specific sciences. *Science,* **176**: 1203–1210.

Taub, E., I. A. Goldberg, and P. Taub. 1975. Deafferentation in monkeys: Pointing at a target without visual feedback. *Experimental Neurology,* **46**: 178–186.

Thom, R. 1975. *Structural Stability and Morphogenesis: An Outline of a General Theory of Models,* translated by D. H. Fowler. Reading, Mass.: Benjamin.

Thompson, R. F. 1967. *Foundations of Physiological Psychology.* New York: Harper and Row, p. 127.

Thompson, R. F., and W. A. Spencer. 1966. Habituation: A model phenomenon for the study of neuronal substrates of behavior. *Psychological Review,* **73**: 16–43.

Toulmin, S. 1972. The mentality of man's brain. In *Brain and Human Behavior,* A. G. Karczmar, and J. C. Eccles, eds. Berlin: Springer Verlag, pp. 409–442.

Von Senden, M. 1960. *Space and Sight,* translated by P. Heath. New York: Free Press.

Waddington, C. H. 1957. *The Strategy of the Genes.* London: Allen and Unwin.

Wheeler, J. A. 1975. At last—a sane look at the "arrow of time." *Physics Today,* **28**: 49–50. (A review of P. C. W. Davies' *The Physics of Time Asymmetry.*)

Whorf, B. L. 1956. *Language, Thought and Reality*, J. Carroll, ed. Cambridge, Mass.: MIT Press.

Wiesel, T. N., and D. H. Hubel. 1974. Ordered arrangement of orientation columns in monkeys lacking visual experience. *Journal of Comparative Neurology*, **158**: 307–318.

Wittgenstein, L. 1953. *Philosophical Investigations*. Oxford: Blackwell.

_____. 1955. *Tractatus Logico-Philosophicus*. London: Routledge and Kegan Paul.

_____. 1958. *The Blue and Brown Books:* Preliminary studies for the "Philosophical Investigations." New York: Harper and Row.

Wynne, L. C., and R. L. Solomon. 1955. Traumatic avoidance learning: Acquisition and extinction in dogs deprived of normal peripheral autonomic function. *Genetic Psychology Monographs*, **52**: 241–284.

Subject Index

Name Index